IN SEARCH OF ETHICAL LEADERSHIP

By Torin M. Finser

In Search of Ethical Leadership
School Renewal
School As a Journey

In Search of
Ethical Leadership

IF NOT NOW, WHEN?

Torin M. Finser, Ph.D.

SteinerBooks

Published in the United States by
SteinerBooks
PO Box 799, Great Barrington, MA 01230

www.steinerbooks.org

Library of Congress Cataloging-in-Publication Data

Finser, Torin M., 1956–
  In search of ethical leadership : if not now, when? / Torin M. Finser.

    p. cm.
Includes bibliographical references.
  ISBN 0-88010-532-1 (alk. paper)
  1. Waldorf method of education. 2. Leadership—Moral and ethical aspects.
3. Moral education. I. Title.

  LB1029.W34F54 2003
  370.11'4—dc21

                                                      2003012830

              10 9 8 7 6 5 4 3 2 1

Contents

To my Parents,

Ruth and Siegfried Finser,

In Gratitude

Acknowledgments

For this work, as with many other aspects of my life, my wife has been my Muse, always ready with new inspiration and willingness to share reflections. I am grateful for my colleagues, especially Arthur Auer, who is a walking treasure-trove of wonderful resources and ideas, not to mention constant colleagueship. Nicky Heron has again served as my most amazing editor—she was able to get inside the meaning of my words, rearrange paragraphs, make suggestions, and through dialogue, add her wisdom to the manuscript. And finally, I thank those who have read my previous books and have given me constant encouragement to continue writing!

Preface

In the years after the tragedy of Columbine, my attention, like many others who care about the state of education, was drawn to the issue of violence in schools. It is unnecessary, unacceptable, and preventable. In schools dedicated to forming our future citizens, can we not do better? Surrounded by caring adults, counselors, coaches, and many others, how did we fail to notice and fail to help those who ended up committing such crimes? What changes do we need to make to prevent future instances of school violence?

Unfortunately, the years that have followed prove that we still have not found any easy answers to these questions. I quickly became disillusioned with simplistic answers to the problem, such as: We need more guidance counselors. The perpetrators were abandoned children, often victims themselves, who needed better homes and parenting. Class sizes were too big. We did not have the resources. All these things are true, but they left me dissatisfied, because they seemed to address the symptoms and outer layers, but not the core issues.

We can start to address these core issues by looking at the fundamentals of good schools, such as the quality of teaching, the curriculum, architecture, and community dynamics. Further, if education shapes a person's life for years to come, we need to ask what we are doing to prepare future leaders. And what kind of leadership do we need? In discussing the Israel-Palestine conflict with a student, I found myself asking, "Why has this been going on and on, year after year? When will everyone have enough of this senseless violence? What will it take to bring about real peace in the Middle East, as well as other places around the world?" And my student's matter-of-fact response to my impassioned outburst was, "We need a Gandhi."

The response from my student brought up a host of other questions around leadership, framed in part by recent ethical lapses in the Catholic Church, the Olympic Committee, and businesses such as WorldCom and Enron. With so many "well educated" people in charge, what happened to ethical standards? How can such smart people commit such horrendous crimes? What do we have to do to find, develop, and support ethical leadership? If we cannot clone a Gandhi, what can ordinary people such as you and I do in the search for ethical leadership?

My questions started me on a path of inquiry whose end result was not immediately revealed. My research process has been like following the ancient Greek hero Theseus through the labyrinth in search of the bull-headed monster known as the Minotaur. Aridadne gave Theseus a magical ball of twine to assist him in his quest. Like Theseus, I too have followed the thread, and it has taken many twists and turns before eventually leading to the Minotaur. I never considered the more traditional method of articulating some hypothesis and then finding the data to make my case. For me, traditional, quantitative research methodology, by itself, is too abstract, does not allow the possibility of finding connections that might otherwise be glimpsed, and is less exciting. So the approach I used has been more chaotic, but it demonstrates the process of a path of inquiry in searching for answers rather than proofs. This path of research ended up mirroring the results; holistic solutions are better achieved through person-centered inquiry. In other words, statistics do not answer the problem of ethics, for you cannot remove humanity from the equation. I have come to realize that everything we do—even the way we ask questions and go about the small chores of daily living—influences the desired outcome. Such methodology is less than predictable, but it is nevertheless filled with the potential for creative solutions to the problems we face.

Experience tells me that this is how we live our lives. We may wake up in the morning with some idea of what we intend to do, but each day is like a little boat floating on the stream of life. The turns, eddies, and rapids bring unexpected encounters; we meet people, have a chance conversation, receive a phone call, or happen to glance at a page in a book. These moments jump out at us; our little boat adjusts and takes a new course. I have learned to respect this process, for, in it, destiny can be more active. Appointment books are not the only determining factors in our daily lives. There is a spiritual aspect to this synchronistic process that puts us in touch with something greater than ourselves. There is more at work: our actions, even those from the distant past, can affect the present moment. The question is, are we awake enough to perceive it?

The first step in my journey of discovery came when I attended a conference in Flensberg, a small town in Germany near Denmark. I travel outside the United States once or twice each year in an effort to connect my work as director of Waldorf teacher training with those of my international educational colleagues—in this case a group of people exploring the issue of freedom for education. In addition to politicians, teachers, administrators, and parents, I met a delegation of teachers from Russia. They had a fascinating story to tell, which I heard in an informal meeting following the conference.

The scene was a living room in a small apartment on the coast of the Baltic Sea. We nibbled refreshments and tried to make polite conversation, which was not easy in a group of people who spoke several different languages. To understand the Russians, I related my questions to an English-speaking German, who relayed them to another person, who translated them into Russian. Their answers came back by the same circuitous route. In spite of these language barriers, I learned about the "Beautiful Schools" movement in Russia.

The Beautiful Schools movement is a network of hundreds of schools in which people are committed to the notion that the environment serves as a major influence on learning. The members of the delegation cited Dostoevsky: "Beauty will save the world." These schools are, for the most part, public schools built during Stalin-era, Soviet Russia, a time not known for its architectural achievements. In fact, without any governmental assistance, these volunteers are changing the environments of many schools. They described how parents and teachers had, one by one, started to transform the ugly, gray buildings into places worthy of children. Their efforts were often quite simple, beginning with cleaning and painting rooms, rearranging furniture, putting artwork on the walls, and planting gardens. From there, they began to study different forms of lighting, classroom supplies, and other interventions that could improve the quality of students' lives. All this has been accomplished with little or no money, other than what was donated by parents and teachers.

The encounter with the Russian delegation and their story made a deep impression on me. Upon my return to New Hampshire, I began to look into the relationship between school architecture and learning. I was interested in establishing a connection between aesthetics and self-esteem. If this could be demonstrated, then it would be much easier to show how self-esteem influences student learning and achievement positively.

It was shortly after my visit with the Russians that a colleague gave me a book by Christian Rittlemeyer, *Schulbauten positiv gestalten: Wie Schuler Farben und Formen erleben* (roughly translated, "Experiencing the positive in school buildings: How students experience forms and color"). Rittlemeyer uses psychological studies and photography to show the responses of children to different school buildings. (Some of his findings are described in chapter two.) This was the second piece of the puzzle and just the kind of research I was looking for! Without a doubt, children respond positively to certain kinds of architecture and not to others. They respond decisively to beautiful school buildings and are put off by others, saying that they could spend time, focus, learn, and socialize better in aesthetic environments. And this was not merely a matter of opinion— the results were remarkably consistent among various ages in a variety of locations. Beautiful schools, it seems, do matter!

At that point I started looking at schools differently. Many are made of cinder block, concrete, and other drab materials. Often, the roofs are not quite flat. The shape of most buildings is rectangular or square, and there is a heavy feeling to them. The classrooms are often much worse. Low ceilings, clutter, and overcrowding are the first impressions. Then one starts to notice the fluorescent lighting, antiseptic smells, and synthetic materials. The bulletin boards and walls are often full of half-finished projects, so-called art work, and charts of dated events. For example, one room had posted material on the presidential election that had happened six months previously. The air in some rooms is spent, used up, smelly, and a few rooms had no natural lighting.

In contrast, the School of the Roaring Forks, a Waldorf school in Carbondale, Colorado, is a building that is constructed with an environmentally friendly system of hay bales.[1] Compressed and then coated, the hay bales are relatively inexpensive and the main building was put together by parents and teachers over a weekend. The entrance is inviting, with a display of colorful student work on the walls. The classrooms are each painted with a different, age-appropriate color, which is typical in most Waldorf schools. So, for instance, the first grade is red and the second and third grades flow from orange into yellow and green. Student work—paintings, maps, arithmetic exercises, and form designs—sparkle on the walls and bulletin boards. There is an abundance of natural lighting, with many windows and doors that open to the changing natural world outside. Students have

---

1. See Laurie Guevara-Stone, "Better than Bricks: A School Built of Straw," *Mothering,* no. 116, Jan/Feb. 2003.

made the playground structures, and there is a feeling of joy and active learning in the school. Built with minimal cost and community participation, the school in Carbondale could be the story in every town. So, why is it the exception?

The next phase in my journey took place in Greece. During a brief sabbatical trip in the spring of 2002, after years of gazing at photos and reproductions, I finally got to see the famous temples. Far out on Cape Sounion stand the remains of the temple of Poseidon. Perched upon a knoll overlooking the blue Aegean Sea, its columns rise in full clarity and beauty against the sky and sea. Despite the passage of time, there is something enchanting, even haunting, about this particular temple. The stone foundations are simple, the carvings not unusual, yet the sixteen Doric columns sing with the interplay of light and air. I felt as though my humanity was directly connected with earth and heaven as I experienced what stood before me. There was a clear streaming, a kind of breathing, between above and below, and I felt a lightness and joy in beholding the temple.

Then it came to me. This unity of below, middle, and above— or in the symbolic language of Greek mythology, the Underworld of Hades, the Earth of Demeter, and the place of the Gods on Mount Olympus—this harmony of experience is what the builders had intended. We can experience our humanity in these buildings as the design is one of lightness and air, and thus it belies the weight of the material used; architecture has overcome the weight of gravity. In these sacred spaces, we as human beings are given the room to think, feel, and consider our actions on this earth.

In contrast to the Egyptian pyramids, when we look closely at the temples of ancient Greece we see that the foundation, columns, and roof are balanced, each in wise proportion to one another. So I considered that, if a temple represents the complete human being, there must also be a correspondence in the parts of the temple to the parts of the complete human being, as suggested by those who have worked with the indications given by Rudolf Steiner (1861–1925), founder of Anthroposophy. The foundation of the entire edifice is like my body; the roof replicates the heavens as does my spirit; and the columns mediate between the foundation and the roof, as my soul does between my spirit and body.

To me, the harmony of the Greek temple at Sounion symbolized my own being's striving for wholeness. While on the bus back to Athens, I thought of some of the schools I've described here. Which aspects of this harmonious Greek temple predominated in school buildings, and which were lacking? In my experience at least, most school buildings today in North America and abroad are exaggerated foundations. That which properly belongs to the foundation—poured concrete and rectangular stone—is pushed up into the walls. There is little of the "column" (the middle, striving element). And the flat roof shows that the third portion, the symbol of the heavens, is cut off entirely. If architecture represents an image of the archetypal human, then our school buildings are bodies with little soul and spirit. The higher aspects of our humanity are suppressed into physicality.

When I pay attention to my breathing, it reveals the truth and offers me an answer—if I am aware of its language. In the Greek temple, breathing came easily and with joy. In many of the schools I visit, in many parts of the world, it is hard to breathe freely. I often feel cramped, and after some hours I tend to get a headache. For me this is a momentary experience, yet it is what many children have to endure day after day.

If their environment suppresses children's souls and spirits, a kind of pent-up frustration builds over time. Children who have fewer counterbalancing conditions, such as a healthy family life, are the first to crack under the oppression of this kind of environment. Add to this the special sensitivity of some children and the influences of violence in the media, and you have a potent recipe for violence in our schools. Even the children who do not succumb to overt acts of violence suffer as a result of the mindless, unimaginative architecture of many of our schools.

The question then arose for me: What kind of human beings are we growing in these schools?

The fourth stage of my journey occurred when, like many others in America, I read about the events at Enron, WorldCom, and other corporations. I wondered how such "successful," intelligent executives could fall so low. If they had such power, money, and prestige, why did they do it?

I have never been satisfied with the various explanations in the articles I have read. Although we now have a great deal of information, I am still not convinced. Who were these people, really? Articles describe all the things that went wrong in the workplace, but little attention has been given to the educational background and the *Weltanschauung,* or worldview, of the perpetrators. The financial figures, accounting lapses, and indeed much of the reporting I have read reminded me very much of the world in which those leaders worked: a self-enclosed system. We have not been asking the right questions! The media did not question the moral or ethical sense of these situations, but simply treated the problem as one of clever people who did stupid things and got caught. In Martha Stewart's case, the media questioned why she was not careful about the evidence of insider trading, rather than: Did she do it and, if so, why? The media, therefore, helps to perpetuate this kind of unethical system, and this led me to think about the topic of ethics. I began by looking back to Aristotle, then I looked at contemporary books on ethics and started to write down some of my thoughts. I still had no idea where this journey was heading.

One day at a bookstore, I opened a book and read a few lines that jolted me. After many years of cruel torture and imprisonment, Jacques de Molay, the last Grand Master of the Knights Templar, stood in front of the scaffold surrounded by a huge crowd and spoke:

It is right that on such a terrible day, and in the last moments of my life, that I should reveal all the iniquity of lies, and that

I should let the truth triumph; and so I declare, before heaven and earth, and I avow, even if it be to my eternal shame, that I have committed the greatest of all crimes.... But this is my crime: that I have agreed to the accusations brought with so much malice against an Order which truth forces me to recognize today as innocent. I gave the declaration demanded of me only to escape torture and suffering, and to move to pity those who made me suffer. I know the torments endured by those who had the courage to revoke such confessions, but the terrible spectacle before me cannot make me confirm a first lie by a second. In such a wretched state I renounce life willingly; it is already only too hateful to me. What use to me are such sad days, when I have only earned them by lies. (Howarth, p. 17)

Shortly after these words were spoken, the king—ironically named Philip the Beautiful—gave the order for the last Templars to be burned at the stake. Who were these men who had such a strong sense for the truth and would not save their lives by lying to please the king and Pope? Here were leaders, it turned out, who were ahead of their time. They had tremendous wealth, but renounced all personal possessions; had great influence for many years, yet were not formal leaders; and were powerful enough to elicit the envy of the king of France. On Friday, October 13, 1307, at the crack of dawn, all the Templars in France were seized and placed under arrest by the king's men. Their property was immediately confiscated. Some escaped, many were summarily tried and killed, others languished in prisons for years. The last Grand Master was burned at the stake in March of 1314. This story led me to a passionate exploration of these remarkable knights of the Middle Ages. Intuitively, I sensed a deep connection between the terrible events at Columbine, the effects of school architecture on students, the current crisis in ethical leadership, and the Knights Templar.

Because I was willing to follow my intuition, my soul was open to the inner voice. At the beginning of my journey I saw only the tapestry, but as I continued my journey, the thread—

the gift of Ariadne to Theseus—became apparent. I gradually began to see the thread of ethical leadership. As you journey through this book, may you find your own thread and discover for yourself what it means to act ethically in leadership situations. As seen in the speech of Jacques de Molay, ethical leaders are self-aware, inwardly active servants of a higher order of human development. They work with destiny and shape communities of the future. This book is meant for all those who care about our modern condition and to encourage them to take hold of this moment of human destiny, to speak with a clear voice, and to uphold what is true, beautiful, and good in this world.

Torin M. Finser
2003

1. The Leadership Challenge

THE LEADERSHIP TRAGEDY OF 9/11

The tragedy of 9/11 is a powerful example of the leadership challenge. Never before in our country have so many innocent people lost their lives in a terrorist act. It was a defining moment for our nation. Those who lost their lives on September 11 did so as a complete sacrifice. They had not signed up for military service to wage war against terrorist groups, nor had they decided to fight a global battle. They were simply living their lives, going to work and sharing time with family and friends. Their unexpected death was a sacrifice in every sense of the word, and the result was the creation of a huge pool of spiritual capital for the United States.

By "spiritual capital" I mean a form of abundance born out of sympathy, love, and compassion. All over the world, people of different cultures and nations united because of the tragedy that day. This outpouring of world empathy created spiritual capital, just as financial institutions hold monetary capital. This kind of capital, however, is held not by institutions but by the soul life of humanity.

In the days immediately following September 11, our political leaders framed the issues in such a way that the course of action was set on a specific track, one that led to Afghanistan and subsequently to another war in Iraq. If the issue had been framed differently from the start, and if our leaders had understood the special opportunity at hand, much could have been accomplished. For instance, the President could have said to the nation:

This tragedy was largely the result of the unresolved conflict between Palestine and Israel. Because world leaders have failed to heal this long-standing rift, 3,000 people lost their lives, in New York City, in a field in Pennsylvania, and at the Pentagon in Washington. Rather than go to war, we will wage peace as never before. I call upon the United Nations and the Security Council to join us in imposing a peaceful settlement in the Middle East. Let us use our moral outrage to stop the conflict at its roots. Let the members of the Security Council draft a peace proposal within thirty days and bring it to a vote in the General Assembly. If agreed to, let us use our combined military, diplomatic, and moral authority to implement this accord in the Middle East. For instance, every nation that has expressed outrage at what happened at the Twin Towers will be expected to contribute peacekeepers, which if necessary will outnumber the combatants. We will then bring people together in special rebuilding projects that will train skills in cooperative living. With peace in this region, we can feel secure that one great breeding ground for terrorists has been eliminated. We have countered terrorism with peace and fear with security. Let us act together, so that those who died on 9/11 will not have died in vain. Let us show that we will not respond in kind, but that our outrage will be channeled into new authority to overcome injustice and oppression wherever it may be. We are greater than our adversaries.

Of course, this is not what was said, and we see how our standing in the world has diminished. The fight against terrorism is losing focus, and conflict in the Middle East continues. We have ousted the Taliban in Afghanistan, but Al Qaeda and their lackeys have simply moved to other countries. We cannot win a game of global blind-man's buff. New terrorists are being recruited and trained, and there will always be new suicide bombers available if we allow the Middle East crisis to continue.

This is the second tragedy that occurred in the months following 9/11. Instead of using that hard-earned spiritual capital to exercise new authority to counter oppression, world hunger, global pollution, injustice, and conflicts in the Middle East and elsewhere, political leaders used the outpouring of support to bomb Afghanistan, increase surveillance of ordinary citizens, and strengthen governmental authority. Our leaders did not appreciate the real opportunity. Many took the low road of revenge, military might, and superpower hegemony. The tragedy was that we could have accomplished so much more, had our leaders been able to exercise the moral authority made possible by the tragic events of 9/11.

Why did we squander this spiritual capital? Our leaders were not up to the task. They did what was popular in the moment and gave in to the basic human instinct for revenge. As with certain business CEOs, many of our politicians were simply unable to practice ethical leadership. As my student said, we need a Gandhi or a Martin Luther King, someone who can speak across the divisions, not into them. Instead, we are still stuck in an ever-moving war we cannot win as long as we use the wrong weapons.

The overriding need today is for an awakening of moral sensitivity that is modeled by our political, business and church leaders. I suggest that educators, parents, scholars, and those seeking our votes in future elections open a dialogue on how to cultivate such ethical leadership. This is what our country so desperately needs if the victims of 9/11 are to be truly honored. Following are some other examples of Leadership Challenges that can be used to begin such a dialogue.

EXAMPLES OF LEADERSHIP CHALLENGES

Scenario 1: A hypothetical, late evening conference call involving the top dogs of Business Incorporated: all members of the "Executive Committee," including Jack, the CEO; John, the attorney; Sue, the secretary; and Sam, the accountant.

Jack: Are we all here?

Chorus: Yes.

John: Officially, of course, I am not participating.

Jack. Yes, as usual. Now, have you all had time to look over the proposals we sent out?

Sue: Yes, it seems like a clever solution to the third quarter reporting problem. John, is it kosher?

John: You mean legal? Well, as with all the other proposals we've okayed lately, the beauty of this is that there are no specific laws against this. The SEC has never litigated, either.

Sue: You mean no one has ever thought of it before?

John: Yes. Clever, eh?

Jack: All I know is that the third-quarter numbers need to look good. Do whatever you have to, John. And Sam, at our next "unofficial" conference call, let's review those severance packages. I'd like to increase the numbers for each of us, just a few million apiece, just in case this thing blows up.

John: No chance. Most shareholders don't read these financial reports anyway, and the people that do read them are all on our payroll as consultants. We just need to keep those share prices up.

Notice that there was no serious discussion of the substance of the "proposals," no questioning of the accountant, and no thought of the shareholders, consumers, or the ethics of the move in question. Can we call these people leaders?

Scenario 2: It was 6:30, past the scheduled adjournment time, and the meeting of faculty, teachers, staff, and administrators of a Waldorf elementary school was still in session.

It was the last meeting of the year and they had yet to find someone to serve as chair of the faculty beginning in September. The atmosphere was tense, since everyone knew all the candidates they did not want, but few could be found who were both acceptable and capable. In the end, the meeting concluded in frustration and without a decision. They chose not to take the time to work through their problem, and so the school went into the summer with no clear leadership structure—only a few sketchy ideas about a summer administrative committee, membership unknown. Where are the leaders our schools so desperately need?

Scenario 3: You are traveling and have a toothache. Suspecting that a filling fell out and, with the pain becoming acute, you locate a dentist and schedule an appointment.

When you arrive, a warm, friendly receptionist greets you and hands you the necessary paperwork. While standing at the counter, however, you are dismayed to hear her say, "Robert is a wonderful man. All his patients love him. Although he still has not completed his dental training, he knows when to ask for help. He is on the way toward becoming a great dentist and has made very few mistakes. He was elected the most congenial member of his high school class. You will soon see why."

Would you stay to have your tooth filled? Especially after you discover that the dentist he consults with while learning the job lives 300 miles away? Does it really matter that he was elected to something in high school? Are you more concerned about his popularity or his professional expertise? What if you become one of his "few mistakes?"

Most of us would not accept an untrained but likable person as a dentist; yet why do we accept this kind of person for our school professionals? We have untrained teachers in the classroom, and many unprepared leaders facilitating meetings, serving on the board and leading our schools. How many faculty chairs, board presidents, and committee chairs selected this past year have had adequate preparation for their job? I know that I was unprepared when I was first asked to serve as faculty chair. Why do we have high professional expectations for dentistry, engineering, surgery, and electrical work, but not for education? Where is our investment in leadership for our children and our future?

Scenario 4: An administrative situation in a Waldorf school (representative of such self-administered private schools in many countries around the world).

This Waldorf school had a highly competent administrator who resigned after five years of service. Many had appreciated his hard work, professionalism, and ability to balance the needs of parents, teachers, and board while getting things done. Yet some had come to resent his "influence" among key donors and board members. So the college of teachers elected to find a more low-key person, someone who would simply carry out their decisions. They restricted the job description of the new administrator, as a result of which he quickly began to feel useless and soon resigned.

Another Waldorf school had such an aversion to any kind of leadership that they opted out and decided to have no leaders. Instead, they created committees. Even after several days at that school as a consultant, I was still discovering new committees: the faculty chair committee, the college chair committee, the agenda committee, the festival committee, the administrative committee, and more. It seemed that the most important group was the ombuds committee, charged with sorting out the conflicts between various committees and individuals.

As a consultant, I could tell many such stories, but these examples illustrate the leadership challenge we have in our schools, framed increasingly by a national and global crisis in business, politics, and even the church. So in my search for ethical leadership these questions arose:

1. Why is leadership in general so often misunderstood?

2. How can we support leaders and others who show initiative?

3. What constitutes ethical leadership?

LEADERSHIP PHOBIA

Why is leadership in general so often misunderstood? As Tom Wren observes in "James Madison and the Ethics of Transformational Leadership," ever since our independence as a nation, there has been a conflict between our values of equality and authority (Ciulla, p. 65). This has played itself out in the ongoing struggle of the prerogative of the President versus Congress, our love of public education and experimentation with private schools, as well as in the tensions of organizational life. We cannot seem to decide—are we a hierarchy or a team? We worship individuality and individual achievement in sports, business and entertainment, yet we often root for the underdog, support equal pay for equal jobs, and call ourselves a democracy. We try to exercise our freedom to vote, yet give away extraordinary power to the President in times of war. We often profess to be more egalitarian than we are, and our language often outpaces our actions in regard to democracy. So for example, we "liberate" a country only to make deals with others that have long been dominated by dictators. We are selective in our support of democracy and human rights.

Our schools are a microcosm through which we can view ethical leadership issues. Schools often put themselves through all sorts of contortions just to avoid placing responsibility and/or authority in leaders. Structures are created to provide a safety net, in case anyone exercises too much leadership, and the emphasis is often on the circle, found in statements such as "we all take responsibility," which is often an invitation for no one to take any real responsibility. Committees are created, communication is diffused, and real authority often stays with the group, whether a board, faculty, or college of teachers.

Now don't misunderstand me; groups can be very effective, and I am not advocating dictatorship. I am pointing to a tendency in our schools and elsewhere to use the group to obscure responsibility so that in the end, there is diminished ego experience. This is particularly true on the corporate level, as we often have no idea who is making the decisions that are affecting every facet of our lives. In a school environment, this suppression of leadership can have the effect of pushing human dynamics down to the level of the emotional life, with many personal feelings and agendas at play instead of the objective needs of the school. This in turn can lead to a variety of the social problems I will describe.

An example of this lack of responsibility may be seen when parents receive letters signed by "the faculty" instead of an individual. Or the phrase "we have decided" can lead to an us-versus-them feeling by those who are not part of "us." In many not-for-profit organizations, I have found it ironic that leaders often use exclusive language, even when asking parents, board, and faculty to work together to fund-raise or boost enrollment. Yet, unless all adults in the school community feel emotionally and spiritually invested in the school, it is hard to realize concrete aims such as enrolling new families. The inner dynamic often lives under the surface in a school and is not always conscious, but should not be underestimated.

We also have a generational condition that influences poor leadership support. Many teachers and parents in our schools today grew up in a time when Vietnam, Watergate, and other traumatic events fashioned attitudes toward leaders in public life. For good reason, leaders were suspect, and there were many who participated in enthusiastic demonstrations against the establishment. Even today, many think of leadership in terms of the military command-and-control stereotype. We carry around old-fashioned attitudes toward leadership that influence how we work together in our schools and other areas of life.

Ann Charles, former chair of AWSNA (Association of Waldorf Schools of North America), once wrote me a note about "followership," which she feels is a key ingredient in exercising leadership. She noted that leaders can succeed to the extent that they receive the right kind of followership. What does it mean to follow? Do we give ourselves away and become automatons, robots, and spineless by following? Certainly we have instances in history when people suspended critical thinking to follow a political leader. A School, however, is a cultural institution, an entirely different kind of entity. Here, we need to discover talent and capacities that can be supported, much as an audience would support the performance of an exceptional violinist. When I listen to a gifted musician, I follow with heart and soul. But I do not give over my ego. Rather than becoming a slave, I usually step up to a higher level of being, just as I do by supporting leaders who provide for the good of the whole rather than for themselves and a few cronies. Being willing to follow and support the good of the whole can add a spiritual dynamic to adult relationships.

Lets look at this more closely. You have probably been to a beach and enjoyed walking in someone else's footprints in the wet sand. With six children, I have had the pleasure of walking in various sized footprints over the years. It is a wonderful experience. Placing my foot in the sand print of a child gives me a sense of the whole person, from the round dimple of the toddler to the long, slim imprint of the teenager. I have practiced walking in the steps of others—not just on a beach—and it has helped me appreciate people in a new way. By supporting good leaders and not always needing to be in the forefront, we learn more about what a good leader is, and we have the space to look at the larger picture of issues and problems. Thus followership can heighten awareness.

When practiced in a school, where each adult is seen as a leader, followership adds a spiritual substance that feeds every one. For example, tasks need to be delineated, job descriptions made clear, and mandates given. But the art of followership is the practice of supporting leadership. Even the way you listen or read this material right now, in this moment, lends itself to creative support. When we understand someone else almost as intimately as ourselves, we allow freedom, and both become free. Rather than thinking subjective thoughts about other people, we can devote our efforts to imagining their thoughts. As individuals, we can carry someone else in our thinking. This requires a clear lens of perception as well as the ability to follow the thoughts of another person. Freedom comes when this effort

results in less subjectivity and defensiveness, and more proactive empathy.

Another reason leaders are often not supported is that we
project our fears onto anyone who appears in a leadership role.
The behavior of a parent or teacher toward a faculty or college
chair may, in some instances, have little to do with the actual
person in that role, but the position may evoke memories of earlier trauma that now plays itself out in the relationship within
the school. I am not just talking about child abuse, which obviously influences attitudes toward gender and authority. And I
am not just describing Sam's experience with his baseball coach
or Vivian's mean piano teacher. On a more subtle level, we are
influenced by what we read and eat and even how we sleep.
These subtler aspects of our lives affect us just as much as our
past. I often know I am going to have an argument or difficult
encounter hours before it actually happens. Why is that? Why
do we sometimes feel like we got out of the wrong side of the
bed on a given day? It has to do with the riddle of the soul, the
subtler influences in our lives, and what we carry with us into
every human encounter.

And this leads me to one last characterization of why the concept of leadership is often not supported enough. Most of the
people I meet are striving human beings; they are in the process
of development. When one has had colleagues, as I have, for
over twenty-five years, it is wonderful to see how so many have
changed, become more skilled, and taken up new tasks. The
path of a Waldorf teacher is particularly ideal for growth and
development, because they move with their students from
grade to grade. Therefore, they constantly have to learn new
curricula and are in a learning process themselves. Yet, when it
comes to administration, we run into problems. We tend to volunteer for tasks that will help us develop, because we want to
acquire new skills, even in administration. But in this realm, the
dynamics are different than they are in the classroom. Parents,
colleagues, and board members are often not as forgiving as the

children are. When we make "learning mistakes" in administration, the damage can undermine the entire organization. For instance, if the board consists of well-meaning but otherwise financially challenged people, decisions about tuition, scholarships, salaries, and deficits can go from bad to worse very quickly. Simply hiring a competent administrator or business manager, as many schools do, will not make up for the lack of professionalism in the school's decision-making bodies. In fact, I often see a split between those who are less than competent but have the authority, and those who have professional skills yet have circumvented responsibility. According to a recent DANA survey, the average tenure of a Waldorf school administrator is about two years. Consequently, we sometimes find leadership phobia, because those in responsible positions do not deserve to be there.

SUPPORTING LEADERSHIP

We have seen examples of why leadership is often misunderstood; now let us consider the second question: How can we support leaders and others who show initiative? The following are suggestions for providing support for leaders.

1. Develop circles of trust. There are countless ways to do this, but my favorites include an exercise that involves sharing research questions in a school setting; using more complicated methods, such as biography exercises (whereby each person learns more about the others); cooperating in artistic work; and practicing community-building exercises. When a community comes together for a common goal, such as prohibiting overdevelopment or building a community park or recreational facility, people get to know one another—they see individual abilities, and the level of trust builds. Trust develops in a communal setting, not in isolation.

2. Leaders need to develop the ability to see individual capacities more clearly, assign tasks accordingly, and strive for

renewed objectivity toward themselves (as already described in relation to followership).

3. Welcome initiative as a vehicle for future leadership. Anything, even as small as a display on the bulletin board, can be seen as a step in the leadership path. If such an act meets with encouragement, constructive feedback, interest, and appreciation, it is more likely to be followed by others. There are many questions living in the soul life of the one taking the initiative, often simultaneously: Is this necessary? Is it wanted? Am I going too far with this? Is it worth my time? What will others think? The soul is delicate, and even a slightly jarring experience from the outside world can color all future contributions. So we need to see each action, each suggestion, each initiative as a hesitant, sometimes awkward step up the ladder of leadership development. Successful experiences on that ladder will provide rich rewards in leadership potential in any organization.

4. Provide leadership training and mentoring with the same level of commitment and professionalism that we expect in medicine, business, and education. As a society, we value the initial degree, but often fail to provide professional support and mentoring afterward.

5. Know who you are—individually as a person, and cooperatively as an organization. This is not just a prescription for success in businesses such as Coca Cola, Microsoft, and other large companies; it also helps build congruity between the organization and those who work in it. Individuals bring intentions to the workplace, and when those intentions are met harmoniously by the intentions of the organization as a whole, there is a possibility for real alignment and creative productivity.

AXIS OF INVOLVEMENT

In answering the third question—What constitutes ethical leadership?—it is useful to consider a point of view, rather than coming up with a list of attributes. One approach to is to look at the axis of involvement, moving from the extreme of full engagement to total disengagement. Each has characteristics that we know all too well. Leaders often feel stretched and pulled in different directions, like a rubber band, with little time to replenish. These are often our busiest people and, as we also know, are given ever more tasks, because they obviously know how to get things done.

The engagement pole has the potential for tremendous creativity, human encounter, and accomplishment. Yet it brings with it the shadow side of egoism, chaos, and personal agendas. The other extreme, the pole of disengagement, has the potential for perspective, freedom, and selectivity. Yet it brings the shadows of criticism without taking responsibility, apathy, and a fee-per-service mentality.

How do we find the balance? It is a matter of making many small choices each day. We can look at each issue or situation and ask: What level of involvement does this require? I am astonished to find that I often presume I am responsible for something, or that I have to do something without necessarily having been asked. Yet sometimes, because of lack of time and sometimes by intention, when I simply do nothing and wait to see how things develop, the matter resolves itself through other means. A colleague in Fair Oaks, California refers to this as the "Dumbledore school of management," as practiced in the J. K. Rowling's Harry Potter books. A leader can choose when to swoop in and when to retreat as it becomes clear that others are better able to manage things. In fact, many groups are disabled when their formal leaders do too much.

So it is a constant riddle: Do you lend yourself and lean into involvement, or do you stand back and remain poised to enter when needed? This suggests a third way: a path between over-engagement or under-involvement. I call it the path of humility. The leader is engaged spiritually yet remains inwardly composed. One works to attain perspective while objectively perceiving what transpires. This third way presents the possibility

of insight without risking too much personality, the possibility
of support without directing. With the path of humility, the ethical leader is outwardly present when needed, but otherwise
leads indirectly with questions, summation, and support of
right initiative. Those who sound "presidential," those who try
hard to appear like leaders, are often the ones least capable of
the way of humility. Ethical leaders do not need to manipulate
perceptions; their focus is on the needs of the school or organization, not their own personality. Ethical leaders are inwardly
engaged, even while outwardly invisible at times. Their presence is felt through the actions of others, not through the sound
of a single voice. The achievements of the group are synonymous with the achievements of the leadership. Becoming an
ethical leader requires a spiritual practice or discipline that
maintains humility. True humility is the beginning of solving
leadership challenges.

2. Children & Ethical Leadership

A TALE OF TWO BOYS

John and Ken grew up in the same neighborhood—in fact, on the same street. They went to the same schools and shared some classes, since they were just a month apart in age. Eventually, they vied for the same girls. Both were popular, bright and talented, showing every sign of future promise. Yet this is where their similarities end.

As a young child, John loved to play. Even as a toddler, he could be seen on the floor, playing with his blocks and making up stories by the hour. His parents gave him simple things, such as wooden rings that could be stacked on a pole, a cart with different shapes of wood; a doll made out of an old sock, and later, a Brio train set with bright blue, red and yellow cars. When his older siblings were doing homework, John would ask for some crayons and do his "problems." What his parents noticed most, however, was his ability to imagine his way into an activity, creating as he played. Villages, complete with stores and homes, arose on the rug, and the imaginary people were always busy. Later, when he was of Little League age, John could be seen outside throwing his ball against the garage wall, acting out the style and mannerisms of an assortment of baseball players. When "at work" in this way, John did not like to be interrupted, and his family respected his play.

John entered school at the usual age, yet he did not "wake up" to academic learning as quickly as others. He did not learn to read until third grade, but soon soared way ahead of his peers in both comprehension and the sheer number of books he read. Even driving home from a doctor's appointment, one would see this young fellow sitting in the back seat with a book on his lap. His teachers remarked on John's ability to remember stories, but his spelling was often atrocious.

Socially, John tended to have a few good friends, and was well liked by all, yet he did not like to be the center of attention. He preferred to listen, support others, and contribute to the team, rather than get out in front of others. His was a quiet kind of leadership.

By high school, John was at the top of his classes, and he enjoyed all the extracurricular activities he could manage. His first sweetheart arrived from Kansas when he was in eleventh grade, and they were together through graduation. When he was accepted for early decision at an outstanding college, John turned his attention to after-school work to help pay his way. He was reliable and steady, and people—even those who did not know him very well—turned to John for advice. They knew that he had a strong sense for hearing what was really in the heart of the questioner, and he could always be counted on to counsel friends to follow the high road, do what was right and not just what seemed expedient.

John did so well in college that he was given an award to attend law school, which he did with success. He and Polly met one night in a Thai restaurant, and it was love at first sight. Together they looked forward to settling in a rural town in the southeast.

As mentioned, Ken grew up on the same street and knew John well, but his childhood was quite different. His parents were on the fast track in terms of careers, and so he had more than his share of day-care as a youngster. He, too, loved to play, but not in the same way as John. Ken could take things apart— watches, printers, and jewelry boxes. To his credit, when challenged to make amends, he often succeeded in putting them back together again. His play was influenced by the automatic baby-sitter: the TV. Often, his games became violent, and his characters had the quality of an animation.

When Ken entered school, he quickly learned to read, and yet, once he had mastered the skill, he spent little time with books. His favorite subjects were social studies and, later, psychology. He liked to see how people acted and what motivated them. He still enjoyed taking things apart, but now under the auspices of science. Ken was often described as a bright, clever boy.

In high school, Ken seemed to drift a bit, moving in and out of various interests, not always completing his assignments, doing as much as he could as quickly as possible. He saved most of his home time for computer games, at which he became exceptionally skilled.

Ken did not have a high school sweetheart, but he was always the life of the party. He could tell good jokes and moved easily in and out of the crowd. Some said he would grow up to be a politician. He did, in fact, take some college courses in political science, but he soon gravitated to business and earned his MBA in record time. He seemed intent on making a lot of money.

Twenty years later, the two childhood friends met again, this time in a court of law. The case received national attention, especially when it was announced that John would be the prosecuting attorney. His life had not always been easy in recent years, especially after he and Polly lost their third child in a tragic car accident. Nevertheless, he had gradually earned the respect of those in his district. Thus, he was the natural choice to take on one of the biggest cases of the day, which involved a CEO whom, just months before, had been touted as the next Bill Gates.

Ken, who had indeed risen far and fast, was now charged with an array of violations, from breaking SEC rules to criminal misconduct. Everyone was asking: How could this have happened? There is much we still do not know about Ken that would help answer this question, but looking at the facts of his earlier life, one has to wonder whether he had any sense for telling right from wrong. How could such a bright, successful man fall so fast? Considering both the lack of ethical leadership and the troubles of our schools, it is helpful to examine aspects of childhood that pertain to these two areas. What follows is an attempt to look at a few childhood issues that will need greater attention before our society will have the ethical leadership it so desperately needs.

FANTASY AND JUDGMENT
IN THE EARLY YEARS

A visit to Toys "R" Us and other children's stores can be enlightening. There is so much available! Bright colors and an array of everything from cute and cuddly playthings to large, plastic gym sets. Much of what you see has been thought up by adults who think they know what children want. Unfortunately, many of the plastic toys quickly break, and one has to make another trip to the dump and then restock at the next birthday or sooner. The real problem with many of the toys on the market today is that they leave little room for a child's imagination—they are completely preconceived and packaged.

Some parents try and provide their children with toys that are less formed and more open to a child's fantasy. Parents whose children attend Waldorf schools are especially encouraged to do so. For instance, dolls should not have distinct faces; blocks have irregular shapes; and pictures are done in such a way that they emphasize color over form. This is all part of an attempt to let a child finish the image, instead of imposing an adult's version of what a toy should be. An active life of fantasy supports creativity and the future moral development of children. As we saw in the story of these two friends, John was more fortunate in this regard than Ken.

It is helpful to support good habits in other respects as children grow up, not only in terms of meaningful chores around the house, but also schoolwork. If a story is told, for instance, it is helpful for a child to assist in retelling it the next day, following the narrative truthfully, according to the wisdom of the tale. This requires a kind of inner discipline, because the story provides the direction, not the teacher. Rather than encouraging children in the whims of subjectivity—"I liked this and didn't like that," which is so prevalent today—following the narrative builds the capacity for objective perception, seeing and telling what is there, not what one wants to be there. Later in life, this translates into ethical capacities, such as respect for the true needs of a client and what is actually needed and desired. One has to be self-less when retelling a story and when serving clients. Contrary to mindless worksheets, memory can be developed through remembering the pictures in a good story.

Good habits are also formed when children can experience the right kind of authority, as represented by the adults in their environment. This is particularly important in the years between seven and fourteen, when children need the security that comes from respect. It is wonderful when a child can look up in awe at the person telling an enchanting story or drawing a beautiful picture on the blackboard. This respect for proper authority gives children an understanding of what constitutes authenticity and truth. The physical body needs more than fast food for nourishment, and similarly the moral life of children needs the right experience of authority, which develops a sense for authenticity.

The premature exercise of judgment can be harmful. When children are lectured, given morals as dictums or asked to render "commentary" too early, they shut down their wonder and imagination. I have seen some children who sound much like literary critics—acerbic, witty, and extremely opinionated. They can easily become sarcastic and cynical, which works against ethical development. Why? Because cynicism and witty opinions, by their nature, involve reductionist thinking. Matters are reduced to a caricature of what they are and, thus, can be mocked. This attitude of soul disregards the importance of human beings as individuals and often leads to a feeling of superiority over others. If such sarcastic, cynical trends persist, they can lead to blatant disregard for others and the environment. The attitude becomes one of "Who cares about those stinking little fish if I can make some money drilling for oil?" or "Who cares about the health of a community as long as it doesn't cost me money to dump chemicals in the river?"

If children are able to experience the world as good and beautiful in their younger years, they will be able to find the truthfulness of a situation. If children experience a classroom environment that is consistently attractive and inviting, they begin to develop an aesthetic sense of rightness. This appropriateness will develop in the soul life of the child to become discernment. Over time discernment will enable one to judge good from bad. And most important of all, children who have developed in this manner will have the ability as adults to bestow kindness on other human beings, no matter what their career or profession may be.

ARCHITECTURE AND MORAL DEVELOPMENT

In the preface, I mentioned the Beautiful School movement, which focuses on the influence of the environment on a child's development. I believe this movement is important for the development of ethical leadership. My friend and colleague Johannes Kiersch, who worked with the Beautiful School movement in Europe and Russia, makes an eloquent case for aesthetic considerations in our schools. He further notes how the environment influences students' learning, their sense for truth, and the ability to work responsibly:

> The hollow, ritualistic system of bureaucratic learning, which is still in place at the moment, is past its shelf-life. It promotes indifference and violence in our schools, isolates people from each other, buries valuable traditions, blocks unwarped objective awareness, and instrumentalizes all learning processes for the superficial central purpose of examinations. Everything

that is admirable and valuable, everything that is worthwhile learning emigrates and becomes private. Those who remain are the poorest of the poor who are unable to pay for private education.

The development of sciences since the beginning of the modern age has radically changed the life of civilized mankind, on the one hand by means of discoveries and inventions and their technical and industrial use and, on the other hand, by means of establishing clear criteria for delimiting and defining scientific truths and facts. In this respect, it is the indispensable basis for all learning, even in school. It has, however, had to pay dearly for its progress, namely by abandoning all aesthetic and value-bound qualities of knowledge, or, platonically speaking, by removing the beautiful and the good from the realm of truth. As a consequence of this omission, and this loss ... the contents of learning in schools are of questionable value. Living and learning needs of children and adolescents cannot be satisfied with aesthetically and ethically "neutral" knowledge. (Kiersch, pp. 4–5)

Kiersch goes on to articulate several key points he presented at a conference of the European Forum for Freedom in Education:

The "beautiful school" avoids the reductionistic restriction of natural world images. It works with all conceivable forms of world understanding....The "beautiful school" leads its pupils toward original experience. It is based on the knowledge that perceptions have aesthetic qualities and that these qualities are indispensable for a world understanding that is guided by reason. (*ibid.*, pp. 6–7)

Thus, the aesthetic environment and the degree to which the design and architecture of our buildings support the student's well-being influences their experience of truth. It follows that the way students perceive and experience a school influences their behavior. If child-friendly classrooms and buildings meet the child's inner soul, which yearns for beauty, then learning is supported by a unity of inner and outer experience. Likewise, a school based on more than just a reductionist, utilitarian mode of construction can support the diverse "intelligences" of children, whether artistic or craft-oriented, whether a child is interested in stories and words or more in the abstract realities of music and mathematics. Beauty encompasses a broad spectrum of human intelligence, as the well-known educator and author Howard Gardner notes in his book *Frames of Mind.*

Helmut Fend, a professor at the University of Zurich, has spoken of the importance of school atmosphere, the "ethos" of learning, which is so heavily influenced by buildings and the environment.[1] These are the things that shape children's attitudes and, when done correctly, can help create a relationship culture instead of a me-first mentality. A relationship culture can develop from cooperative learning rather than the test-based system of learning. Similarly, the cleanliness and attention to detail of classroom decor show students the goodwill and care of the adults responsible. When a classroom is beautiful, when attention is given to the color of the walls, when artwork is displayed, and when there are healthy plants in a room, it sends a message to those who spend so many hours there: "We care about your well-being; we want you to feel comfortable, supported and loved." Students in turn can then be expected to take more interest and care of their environment, and this enhances a productive learning climate. Care and consideration can be learned early on, and our classrooms need to provide this kind of ethical environment that will encourage the development of ethical behavior.

Christian Rittelmeyer performed many perceptual-psychological investigations of mental moods that result from various forms of construction, colors, and the type of lighting used in our schools. He confirms the influence of aesthetics upon behavior. Children experience buildings as either inviting and friendly or

---

1. The writings of Helmut Fend include *Eltern und Freunde: soziale Entwicklung im Jugendalter* (Seattle: Huber, 1998).

cold and distasteful. The colors on the walls and the type of lighting can be either calming or enlivening, helpful to learning or distracting, even irritating. Fluorescent lights and "institutional" colors such as pea green evoke negative responses from children, whereas natural lighting and "real" colors, such as pastels make children feel happy. The outside environment and design are also important. Does a school have a garden, various kinds of trees and bushes, imaginative play structures, or is the "yard" just that—a flat surface of asphalt? The type of buildings we use, says Rittelmeyer, influences the psychological makeup of children, which of course, influences learning.

Stewart Brand, in his book *How Buildings Learn*, makes the point that, whereas domestic houses change over the years and respond to a family's needs and hopes, "institutional buildings act as if they were designed specifically to prevent change for the organization inside and to convey timeless reliability to everyone outside.... Institutional buildings are mortified by change" (Brand, p. 7). Brand's book contains many wonderful illustrations of domestic, commercial, and institutional buildings over the course of time, showing how the latter, such as the United States Mint in San Francisco, have not changed, despite earthquakes and fires.

Unfortunately, many of our schools fall into the "institutional" category. That means that despite the changing needs of children or new curriculum offered by the teachers, the architecture does not respond and thus does not support those changes. For example, many public schools today embrace project-based learning, which has proven to be a sound way to support learning of all age groups. Instead of reading about things, discussing abstract theories, and writing reports, children actually build pyramids, yurts, and tepees in a housing unit, or work with water to understand how rivers shape the landscape. Most classrooms and school buildings are not designed to fully support project-based learning, making it harder for teachers and children. Many rooms, for instance, do not have adequate space, running water, or storage, and the grounds in some locations consist of asphalt rather than natural open spaces that allow innovative work with projects. When there is a discrepancy between content and form, tension arises. The hard realities of cinder block buildings oppress children, hindering creativity, imagination, and free play, which are the essence of childhood.

These issues are not just relevant to childhood. Through a gardening project with inmates in California, it was found that they became more and more enthusiastic as they learned to grow their own food. Some inmates, as their prison terms expired, requested help with their own garden projects outside of prison. Most remarkable, when the authorities did a study of recidivism, they found that inmates who had participated in the garden project were much less likely to return to crime after their release. Working with nature, outside of institutional walls, and fostering life forces in growing things for the supper table has its rewards for adults as well as children.

In addition to these considerations, the healthy moral development of our children is influenced by the age-appropriateness of their learning environment. In Waldorf schools, we have found that early childhood classes need to be warm and cozy, with little play corners, silks hung from ceilings and walls to create sheltered spaces, wooden toys, and fabric for "dressing up." As one walks through the grades in a Waldorf school, one is treated to an array of colors: red walls in a first grade, oranges and yellows in second and third, yellow and greens in fourth and fifth, blues in sixth and seventh, and violets to purple in eighth. The red, for instance, accompanies the cheerful expressions of the young first graders. The color sequence is a reflection of the collective consciousness that children carry according to their development.

Children look forward to moving to a new room each year, and most teachers involve the children in all sorts of chores to care for their environment. Most important, the children make things with their own hands, such as wooden spoons and forks in woodworking, scarves and hats in knitting, and even their own textbooks. When studying botany, a fifth grade class will write a text about the fern, draw illustrations, and compose a poem when appropriate. These are added each day to the previous lessons on lichens, conifers, and so on until, at the end of a four-week block of lessons, each student has created a hand-bound book on botany. This establishes a firm relationship with the subject; the child works from a warm "connection" rather than the cold intellect of abstract, published texts. This activism promotes social responsibility later on and a connection between concepts and actions. Along the way, each child develops a special sense for beauty and the innate truthfulness in the world of natural phenomena.

One of the best ways I know of providing character education is through the arts. Rather than seeing music, painting, and drama as just "enrichment," educators need to realize the vital role of the arts in moral development. The arts develop the basis for morality in the soul life of each of us. An artistic foundation in the soul life must be laid before a child is asked to exercise judgment. Premature judgment leads to cold, unfeeling decisions that are disconnected from reality. The arts are the basis for a healthy and sound judgment. Children who do a lot of artistic work are engaged, "warmed" by the joy of an encounter that calls for inner engagement with outer materials. Personal interests and wishes are tempered by the objective reality of clay, color or sound. They learn to work with rather than against the material and to embrace the creative process. In the arts, children are building their ethical future. A society that does not support the arts or protect its natural environment is a society based on the bottom line. Nothing else matters, not even human life. The arts develop creative thinking, which is the basis for a democratic and free society.

THE IDIOT BOX

There is so much literature on the effects of watching TV that I will not attempt to capture its breadth and scope. Rather, I would like to highlight just a few themes before drawing them into the question of ethics.

Television pervades the lives of many children today, because it is a kind of cheap baby-sitter. Unfortunately, many families are in such difficult financial situations that this is often the only perceived solution for childcare. One aspect of a society's ethical environment is the proper care of its children. I know families that are able to provide better care for their children, but nevertheless allow them to sit for hours in front of the tube—in some cases watching movies, in others, one show after another. Once in a while, one of our children will come home from a sleepover and report that they watched two or three movies in the space of twenty-four hours! Often, there is little parental supervision, and many watch PG13 long before they are old enough. Instead of playing outside and getting good exercise, children sit for a whole afternoon like vegetables. They then complain and groan when asked to do chores or any physical activity. They become used to a high-octane diet of entertainment.

Because of the nature of the medium and the content of the shows, children are gradually desensitized. They witness with detachment events and images that would otherwise move us in real life. Injury or death can be devastating in the life of a family, yet there is so much on TV that, after a while, it is seen with only passing interest. As a result, the life of feeling is restricted to a narrow band of sensation, and much of the depth and profundity of life is eliminated. There is less awareness of the more sensitive aspects of human interaction, and children who watch a great deal of TV often find it difficult to listen to adults. In fact, I have found it harder to reach TV-children in school; those who watch many hours become passive, and it is much more difficult to get them excited about learning.

As we all know from the numerous books of educators such as Jerry Mander and Joseph Chilton Pearce, the advertising aimed at children is especially lethal. With great cunning, images and sounds are created to entice, shape, and create desires that never existed before. Children are more susceptible, because they are more open to the world in general; they may start imitating TV characters after just a show or two. Our children become victims of deceptive advertising. According to author Michael Moore (*Stupid White Men*), there is also an alarming commercialization of public schools, whereby Coke or Pepsi or some other multi-national corporation sponsors the band or the football team in order to help subsidize the diminishing public funds going to schools. Signs and clothing bearing corporate logos are given to the school, and vending machines are installed to sell the company product. Thus, kids are indoctrinated very early to be consumers of those products.

All this happens in place of healthy sensory stimulation. Instead of running, playing ball, jumping rope, climbing trees, building forts, creating hide-and-seek games, children sit numbly in front of the box, living in a virtual world. Added to this scenario are video games, play stations, and other electronic media, and children can remain immobile for an entire weekend. Parents are "too busy" to counteract this trend and let things go, often knowing better but unwilling to drop their own activities to go outside to play with their children. Instead of outdoor childhood games, indoor board games, drawing, charades, or baking, our children sit in front of the distorted images of shows that, even they will admit, are generally silly and boring. Worst of all, their senses are not just atrophying, they are being attacked by images and have little or no time to process them effectively. There is a method of camera work that imitates the MTV-style, whereby images are quickly juxtaposed so that there is no time to absorb the information. It is a matter of quantity over quality. Even news shows have two or three things going on at once, with the anchorperson speaking, insets of other events in the corner of the screen, and a running display of breaking events across the bottom of the screen. This makes it impossible to focus and have any real sense of what is happening. Even worse is the violent nature of the medium. Try this experiment: turn on the TV for a few hours on a major network, and count the number of violent acts that occur in just one evening. How can anyone contend that behavior is not affected by viewing constant violence?

Even if TV violence can be avoided, one is then likely to encounter clever sitcoms. We see people doing anything for the sake of a laugh. Mothers and fathers are put down, schools and learning are ridiculed or marginalized, and the dialogue is often so grammatically flawed that it becomes pure nonsense. It is the affect that is always most important. The character's wardrobe or flippant responses have become the focus, rather than the human qualities of faithfulness, honor, or rugged integrity, which may not always be so polished. It's no wonder so many of our teens adopt this same slick, disrespectful attitude toward adults and social truths.

Perhaps most shocking is the number of crime and police shows that continue to air year after year. The world portrayed by such shows is one of might-makes-right, dog-eat-dog, and the continued oppression of groups in low social standing. Although the cops often "win" in the end, their methods and intelligence are valued over wisdom. It is thus always refreshing when one of the characters, such as that played by Angela Lansbury in *Murder She Wrote,* combines folksy common sense and wisdom with plain intelligence. But most of the characters in cop shows are more clever than wise. There is, in fact, little time between commercials for anything like wisdom.

With few exceptions, TV portrays an amoral world. If we consider the statistical evidence of how many hours of television an average child watches, we cannot be surprised by the lack of ethics in the workplace. It is like constantly feeding children candy and then expressing surprise that they become over-weight or diabetic. Our child-rearing practices—from the lack of care in the learning environment to the lack of care in during lei-sure time—have contributed to the present social challenge of ethical leadership.

COLLEGE INDULGENCES

For most young Americans, a college education is a major goal. Studies have shown that a college education is a significant fac-tor in higher lifetime income, and career choices certainly become more plentiful. Yet it is often the prestige and expense of the education, rather than the content, that motivates applica-tions to a particular university. Clearly, students who go to Ivy League schools have an edge on students who go to a commu-nity college and then to a state college. Witness the determina-tion of parents to place their children in the "right" schools, even in the early grades. There was much discussion on TV news shows and in the *New York Times* during the second war in Iraq regarding the economic situation of many of the young Ameri-cans who had recently "volunteered" for the military service. Many evidently volunteer because they lack the funds for col-lege and, likewise, lack job opportunities afterward. It is another symptom of a lack of ethical leadership that some young people are given greater opportunities simply because their parents can pay for an expensive education, while others see the military as their only opportunity.

The value of learning cannot be disputed, and there are many inspirational professors at our colleges who have made a differ-ence in the lives of countless students. The following arguments are thus not intended as an indictment of college education, but to point out the costs, delivery, and general lifestyle on campus.

At a time when many parents are working overtime, college students are living the good life. Visit a typical private college, and you will see a luxurious lifestyle. Walk through the tree-lined paths and manicured lawns, stop in the dining halls, and sample the food—often available all day and into the night. Work out at one of the athletic centers, spend time in the comfort of the library with the latest technology, and attend some of the cultural events—and of course, there are the parties. A student need not attend classes every day and can arrange a few days off each week by using creative scheduling. If you need medical care, counseling, or career services, most colleges have it. It is possible, and sometimes even preferable, to never leave campus, since everything is provided, paid for by a hefty tuition.

Which brings me to what I consider a major indulgence—at $40,000 a year, these students live in Club Med cocoons, while many of their parents scrimp and save for years to make it possible. It is not unusual for parents to save for ten or fifteen years so their children can enjoy a few years of luxury and have the opportunity to go into a profession that will enable them to make large sums of money one day. Education is no longer about learning; it's about access to high-paying careers.

It might be argued, "But don't they deserve it? Should they not have a few good years before life's drudgery sets in? After all, did not many of us benefit from those same colleges?" It is not unusual for parents to want their children to have it even better than they did, and there is some satisfaction in providing this final parental gift. Yet, this is not my objection. Let's look more closely at this indulgent way of life and its influence on character development. One aspect of our leadership crisis arises from the way college life has developed.

Living a soft life, never having to do any real work can weaken the moral fiber of young people. I realize that thinking can be considered work, too, but what about the basics of living, such as cleaning, washing dishes, yard work, and earning money? Some students take work-study jobs, and others have part-time work, and this helps balance their more abstract pursuits. However, for those who do not work, one-sided, abstract learning can set the stage for one-sided development, in which the concepts outpace character development. Sometimes we end up with highly intelligent graduates who can talk their way around any issue with ease, yet lack a basic sense for what is right or wrong. Indeed, I have heard such young intelligentsia take one side of the argument and then, a few minutes later, argue the other side with equal effect. It is almost as if the content is not important, as long as one is able to manipulate the information and sound convincing.

This then sets the stage for future political and business leaders who win people over by the force of persuasion, but lack an inner compass for distinguishing right from wrong. Everything is justified in the name of more votes or higher profits. How you get there does not seem to matter. Thus we had the dot-com bubble in the 1990s, when everything seemed to be going swimmingly—at least for the few at the top. With hindsight, much of the momentum was built on unrealistic future expectations and stock options that evaporated when the share prices collapsed.

But it is more complicated than merely lambasting the indulgences of college life. We need to look at the delivery model itself and see what can be reformed to support ethical leadership. If we look at the life of a of college students in a typical private, four-year college today, the day consists of sleeping in late, attending a class or two, perhaps checking out reserve material at the library, before going on to a leisurely meal at the dining hall, a movie or party, followed by a nightcap back in the dorm. Weekends are less strenuous, since they feature more parties interspersed with an athletic contest of some kind, a run into town, or some time on the slopes. Colleges leave much to the discretion of students, with the rationale that they are learning how to manage. I offer the suggestion that it is perhaps just the opposite that they are learning—that "the world owes me and should take care of me; I do not have to work too hard, because enjoyment is the most important thing" (an early version of stock options).

The delivery model teaches the mismanagement of time, dependence on others, and how to live off the sweat of others with the least personal exertion. Given the fact that many childhood homes lack the necessary character education, and the that elementary and secondary schools give mixed messages at best, college life becomes the icing on the cake, the finishing touch. All this is in sharp contrast to the many who still have to forgo a college education and, for example, work at minimum wages as day-care workers. Even many hourly workers at the most prestigious colleges make atrociously low wages, all the while surrounded by the extravagant lifestyles of the students. Ethical leadership would care more visibly about such social injustice.

Human beings have a threefold makeup of thinking, feeling and willing (as postulated elsewhere in this book and in *School Renewal*). Thus, the healthy development of children should engage all three aspects simultaneously. For example, exciting classes engage the cognitive side, and good debates can stimulate a certain level of feelings. But the emotional development of college students is held within a relatively narrow band of opportunity, and many graduates do not have nearly as much emotional maturity as they have cognitive capacities; just consult some of the partners and spouses of our foremost scholars. What is lacking most is the engagement of the will, the primal force in the soul that helps us do what we must do, even when it is unpleasant or uncomfortable. The will is the part of ourselves that moves us from one place to another; it helps us accomplish things in life, it perseveres, and it exercises intuition. We engage the will when we do real work, exert ourselves physically, and confront real life issues.

Those who do not develop enough will power drift around, moving from one job to another, running when there is a challenge in a relationship, and becoming dissatisfied with "what the world has done to me." Those working with a healthy will, on the other hand, try to change the world. They are the people who were gently supported during childhood and who lived a

warm, rhythmical life. These factors contributed to an integra-
tion of inner impulse and outer action—dependable and
responsible people who are able to follow through on what they
say. You may recall the classic story about Abraham Lincoln's
childhood and his lesson about borrowing books. He loved
books and learning, but his family was very poor and he had to
borrow books from his neighbors. One day he left the books
under the eaves of the log cabin, and unfortunately it rained
enough to soak the books and ruin them. Instead of evading
responsibility, he took a job splitting rails until he had paid for
the books, even though he could not benefit in a material way.
How many students have this strong love for books and the will
power to see such a situation through to the end?

If colleges were to address our societal need for ethical leadership and not merely offer more courses, I would suggest the following reforms:

1. A work-study program required of every student, and
   especially those born with the proverbial silver spoon in
   their mouths. This work-study program would require
   each student to perform practical tasks each day for at
   least four hours. They might include food preparation,
   raking leaves, cleaning, construction, or community service in town. This would have the effect of grounding students, and, because their pay would be comparable to
   similar positions in the marketplace, they would get a
   sense of what it really takes to earn a buck without a college education.

2. The day of a typical student should be balanced between
   this work program, taking courses, and reflective, creative
   time. One might assign each aspect one third of a twelve-
   hour day, leaving a few hours of free time and socializing.
   Thus a typical day might look like this:

   8 A.M. – 12 P.M.: Classes
   12 P.M. – 4 P.M.: Campus and community work

4 P.M. – 7 P.M.:   Recreation and socializing

7 P.M. – I I P.M.:   Reflective, creative time

This last section of the day is just as important as the other sections. We all need time to process, digest, and deepen. If college is just about cramming information, it can lead to intellectual diarrhea. As with food, thoughts need to be processed before they can become nourishment. Likewise, the evening hours might be spent reading, writing, making music, walking, sketching, or just reflecting.

3. Many colleges, particularly those in small rural towns, have become cultural centers. I remember elderly folks from Brunswick coming to audit some of my courses when I attended Bowdoin College. Some schools have music festivals and dramatic productions that are widely attended by local residents. This can be further developed so that colleges no longer belong just to the eighteen- to twenty-two-year-olds, but serve as real community centers. This draws in a more diverse population and allows interactions between the "gray beards" and young people, day laborers and academics, merchants and students of economics. With so many resources going to these colleges, they should not belong only to an elite few.

4. Finally, costs could be drastically reduced. It is unconscionable to charge as much for a year of college as the average Americans earns in a year. The *Wall Street Journal* (Feb. 11, 2003) reported: "Although incomes are rising by only one to two percent in most states, tuition at four-year public schools leapt by twenty-four percent in Massachusetts, twenty percent in Texas and seven percent nationally since the 2001/2002 school year." And this is just public colleges.

As a graduate school professor, I know there are ways to deliver services more cost-effectively. We simply need a stronger public advocacy group to do so. The work-study programs mentioned would, of course, save colleges money, but so would more online administrative services, a reduction of the frills of campus life (such as multiple, underused tennis courts), and less money spent on campus construction and more on scholarships. The Egyptians had their gold-tipped pyramids; we have our college campuses. Saving a few relic buildings for posterity is okay, but we do not need one in every town. Let's get real and cut administrative staffs, ask faculty to teach more, and trade in the campus mall of pub, shops and boutiques for a farm stand of fresh produce.

In fact, college is only a passing moment in the life of those fortunate enough to attend. It is not the be-all and end-all of life. Many alumnae may disagree, but if you look back on life, most people end up in careers that could not have been anticipated, based on their college major. Many find jobs not because of a grade point average, but through the people they meet and their experiences—especially the latter. Internships are given lip service at some colleges and are more real at others. It is life experience that most influences character development. Experience in real life contains inherent checks and balances, positive and corrective feedback, and the responsibility of following through to the end. Colleges can support a broad array of internship experiences so that students sample different career options and meet new people.

As an aside, Antioch College has had a co-op program for many years, demonstrating that they have the right idea about balancing study and work. At the risk of disloyalty (I work at an Antioch University campus), they have the right idea but sometimes fall short on the execution. Sending students away periodically for co-ops tends to create its own imbalance, and some never return to campus to complete their studies. Rather than alternate semesters, I prefer an integrated day approach, in which each day is balanced between study, work and creative reflection. If college life can model a healthy, balanced lifestyle, it is likely that people will continue the same later on in the workplace. For example, learning to manage time, establish priorities, and work with conflict can serve as invaluable tools for an array of future jobs. We need to learn to balance the demands of work and play, stress and relaxation, mental challenge and physical activity.

Spoiling our youth with Club Med college experiences leads to disappointment when real jobs do not support such a wonderful lifestyle. For some, such disappointment can develop into an overwhelming desire for "the good things," no matter what the cost. This urge, combined with the dubious moral education provided in schools and homes, the bombardment of advertising of consumer goods, and the cultural examples shown in the media, can become a lethal mix that leads to "Enronitis." Kenneth Lay of Enron and others wanted to be on the top of the pile, no matter how much deception it took to get there.

Community service, work-study, and a balanced life in college can help prevent these phenomena. Schools are not just about grades, tests, achievement, and future earning power. They are an opportunity to develop good habits, develop aesthetic sensitivity, and support moral development and responsibility so that we have the best possible chance of sending good human beings out into the world.

EDUCATIONAL RELATIVISM

In a review of *Harvard and the Unabomber: The Education of an American Terrorist* by Alyston Chase, Janet Maslin relates the author's theory that the prevalent educational philosophy during the killer's college years laid the groundwork for his later antisocial rage.

> [Chase's] argument has its roots in the philosophy of science that flourished in the aftermath of World War II. In 1945, with the advent of the influential Harvard report titled "General Education in a Free Society," the role of ethics in academia

began to be closely examined. By 1958, when Kaczynski arrived at Harvard as an undergraduate, the Cold War had created covert new links between research and government, links calling for moral blinders that rendered traditional scientific ethics all but obsolete.... From the humanists we learned that science threatens civilization. From the scientists, we learned that science cannot be stopped. Taken together, they implied there is no hope. This split created what became a permanent fixture at Harvard and, indeed, throughout academe: The culture of despair. Chase places a malleable young Kaczynski in the midst of this moral upheaval....

It would help ... if students as bright as the Harvard-era Ted Kaczynski were prized rather than ostracized, and if their work were assessed in terms of absolute morality, rather than the relativism that can so easily be rejected, subverted, or ignored. (*Pittsburgh Post-Gazette*, March 9, 2003)

If everything is relative, and nothing can be considered absolutely true, it is easy to see how vulnerable, volatile individuals can fall into an abyss of despair. Of course, the Unabomber must have had deep-seated psychological challenges to begin with, but his academic years certainly did not help him work them through. In fact, Chase seems to be saying that the situation exacerbated his problems. Even today, the college students in our family come home with stories of how the mythology they were raised with is routinely debunked: King Arthur never existed. The stories that teach lessons and moral issues are of no interest. Anything that cannot be proven is not true, and thus creativity and imagination no longer have any value. Even facts are considered relative, so that the norm becomes a moral climate of great uncertainty that lacks inner standards. The prevailing view is that everything depends on social and environmental influences and on where you stand. An issue can be argued from any side; if you are clever enough, you will win the day and perhaps even a few laughs. Everything is relative, nothing is certain, and ethics is just another theory.

Those who care about the future of our society have a choice: John or Ken; TV parenting or real stories and mythology; beautiful schools or institutions; colleges for the elite or for a democratic workplace; the search for truth or relativism. Each step of the way leads us to countless small decisions that affect our children's lives, which, collectively, add up to what we get back in our experience as a community. Our cultural choices, educational decisions, and child-rearing practices reflect the expectations of our communities. If we wish to begin ethical leadership in the area of our children's lives, we must become conscious of the countless decisions we continually make toward that end.

3. Character Development

If one studies the biographies of CEOs at the companies that have experienced the most serious ethical problems, one is struck by their captivity. They became products of a corporate culture that did not leave them free; their mindset was boxed in, options seemed limited, and dissent was not a serious choice. "[Kenneth] Lay knew about the problems in Valhalla. [David] Woytek had warned him. [Michael] Muckleroy had warned him. Arthur Anderson had warned him. And yet he had heeded none of them because he wanted the profits that [Louis] Borget had promised" (Bryce, p 42). This early incident at Enron is important, because those who tried to warn the CEO and were rebuffed had less incentive to try again. The corporation became even more self-enclosed.

Similarly, some of our business leaders exhibited a profound disrespect for the rights of others—its shareholders and the general public. They seemed to operate from a position of superiority—an illusory summit from which the peons below could be manipulated and deceived. Fair and full disclosure was neglected, obscured, and disregarded. It was as though the Orwellian dictum had been realized: All are equal, but some are more equal than others.

In their pursuit of economic success (not to mention personal financial gain), these same business leaders displayed a singular lack of compassion for those who worked doggedly in the daily business of running a corporation, employees who had risked their pension and retirement savings in the company stock. Deal-making at the top disregarded the destitution that would

visit the employees and their families and the small shareholders. The callous attitude of these CEOs demonstrated a lack of
social responsibility and conscience.

How can we understand such ethical lapses? Those business
leaders were supposed to be the brightest and the best of our
society. Had they not gone to the best schools? Did their companies not reward them with all sorts of perks to enhance the quality of their work? What went wrong?

World War I caused political and social chaos in much of
Europe, both during and after the war. There were revolutions
and regime changes in Russia, Germany, Poland, Hungary, Aus-
tria, and Italy, all of which caused immense hardship and social
turmoil for the citizens of those countries. After the war, historians began to question how it had happened, and who was
responsible. Not only historians, but ordinary people everywhere questioned how it was that such intelligent, well educated men (they were mostly men) could have risen to positions
of political power only to blunder into such a stupid war. Out of
the rubble, further questions were raised about the preparation
and education that produced such leaders. As a result of such
chaos and uncertainty, a successful businessman, Emil Molt,
decided to find a better form of education for the children of his
factory workers. For, after all, our children are our future.

Having been aware for some time of the Austrian scientist and
philosopher Rudolf Steiner, Molt sought him out and asked
whether Steiner might help him open a school for his employees' children. Steiner agreed, with certain conditions: the school
must be open to all children; it must be coeducational; the teachers must be specially trained; and the school must be as free as
possible of governmental control. Molt agreed, and Steiner
called together a group of people he had met over the years—
most of whom were not teachers—and, in August of 1919, gave
them a crash course.

In the weeks before this intensive teacher training, Steiner
delivered several lectures in Dornach, Switzerland, that focused

on the social issues of the time.[1] He talked about materialism, egoism, and miseducation. He called on his audience to delve beneath the superficial treatment of social challenges and to look more carefully at the underlying causes.

If we respond to Steiner's suggestion to look more carefully at the underlying causes of social challenges, an aspect that deserves greater attention is the effect of education on society, in particular how the quality of education during childhood affects adult behavior. We all know that a good education provides a greater chance of success in later life, and those with a college degree usually have higher salaries and access to more career choices. One can say that, in general, everyone supports the notion that education is a good thing. The problem arises when this is translated into a narrow definition of "quality education": good grades, computer literacy, high test scores, and good job placement. Education is usually seen in terms of such restricted outcomes, and, as a result, the reform efforts constrained by this narrow view cannot address larger issues.

An analogy comes to mind in regard to superficial educational goals. An arborist, hoping to produce more apples, makes the mistake of focusing solely on grafting new branches onto an apple tree. Whereas grafting can be successful, one must not neglect the whole tree by failing to provide adequate water and nourishment through the soil or by failing to clear away competing trees or branches that prevent adequate sunlight. Educational reformers today concentrate exclusively on curriculum changes and test results at the expense of a holistic education and the system as a whole.

The thinking behind outcome-based, test-oriented education is the result of natural scientific, materialistic attitudes: If it can be measured, it is good. But the results of a given test must be visible immediately. What if education is more like the apple

---

1. See Rudolf Steiner, *Education As a Force for Social Change*, the six lectures of August 9–17, 1919.

tree, which takes many years to bear significant quantities of fruit? Do we pull up the sapling after three years and give it a "D" because we do not see enough apples? We are much less humane to our children who do not "measure up" than we are to our trees.

Rather than scientific measurement, when we look for the roots of today's lack of ethical leadership, we have to examine education from a different perspective. One way is to move beyond physical interpretation of phenomena to a view based on soul and spiritual realities. As human beings, we are more than the sum of atoms in our body. We have emotions, feelings, ideas, and inspirations. There are aspects that may, in fact, be more intimately related to who we really are than any physical attribute. My clothes and physical health affect me, of course, but my identity, my inner world, cannot be measured so easily or assessed superficially from the outside. To be human is to have not just a physical body, but also a soul and spirit.

In a lectures he gave in August 1919, Steiner spoke of soul transformation. He formulated a holistic philosophy he termed "Anthroposophy." This path of inquiry is intended to help guide teachers in deepening their understanding of human nature, history, and multidisciplinary learning; it was not, however, intended to be taught to students. Steiner observed that, over time, the capacities of a child metamorphose. In Waldorf schools, we have found that education needs to take this factor into account.

A materialist or a test-oriented educator might say: If you impart information on the geography of Ecuador, then a successful student should be able to demonstrate that knowledge in a test or essay, thus demonstrating that the information was retained and can be retrieved. It is a matter of input versus output. In contrast, a psychologist of the soul would look at what happens over time as the child processes that information, and, though this may sound horrifying to many, what is forgotten may be as interesting as what a child remembers. For, as children listen and observe in class, the process of digestion is highly individualized. Some of the best experiences in the classroom may, in fact, not manifest for many years. True capacities need time to mature and develop. For example, the use of imagination in childhood can, with time, become a capacity for creative problem solving—an ability to see multiple possibilities where others remain stuck in narrow preconceptions.

Rudolf Steiner offers several examples of transformed soul capacities:

> Proper imitation develops freedom;
> Authority develops the rights life;
> Brotherliness, love, develops the economic life.[2]

Let us consider these puzzling statements one by one.

"Proper imitation develops freedom." By observing a young child with attentiveness, you can see how readily things are imitated. Start jumping up and down near a five year old, and the child will do the same. Try winding up some wool for knitting, or sweeping the floor or rolling a ball, and the child will soon join in the activity. Young children want to participate and do what they see; they become the environment.

Why are children so imitative? Looking at it from a spiritual point of view, consider the journey before birth, when the child was united with the universe—the spiritual world—where there is no separation as we understand it on earth. A child comes into life predisposed to unite with the surroundings, which places an immense responsibility on adults to offer an environment worthy of a child's imitation. A child's gestures, speech, and habits are formed as a result of what people in the child's environment do. This early absorption helps children learn to function in the world; it is a highly practical process. At the same time, we need to guard them from overstimulation, so that everything that children take in can be firmly processed and assimilated.

---

2. *Education As a Force for Social Change*, pp. 12–14.

Unfortunately, adults are compressing and compromising childhood in general, while the native power of imitation in children is gradually diminishing through benign neglect. The media conspires to propel children into adolescence too soon, and parents often treat a child like "mini-me." As educators Jane Healey, Joseph Chilton Pearce, and many others have documented, children are losing the gift of childhood as they are whisked in and out of cars, exposed to movies far too soon, and overwhelmed by sensory overload. Childhood is being compromised, natural abilities such as imitation are fading, and adults are not spending enough quality time with their children. I know on a personal level what this is all about. When my little Ionas comes running into my office to show me a toy, it is the most important thing in his world. How do I respond? Will it be a perfunctory "Yes, Ionas," as I continue on with my emails, or do I turn and give him my full attention and even get down on the floor and play for awhile? I want him to be a child, sitting on the rug building imaginary villages with blocks and cars, not a mini-adult, imitating my keyboard motions. We need to preserve childhood, for in a child's experience of wonder, joy, and reverence lie the seeds of respect, connection, and ethics for later life.

This loss of childhood borders on the tragic when we consider the transformative aspect of imitation. When properly supported in the early years, imitation can lead to the exercise of freedom as adults. If, as a child, I can unite with the world in appropriate imitation, then I will be grounded in the certainty of existence. When parents offer their children positive actions that can be imitated, children develop positive self-esteem. Later in life, positive self-esteem will give a person the inner security to exercise independence with confidence. Particularly in social interactions, people can work from a sense of inner freedom if imitation has been joined with integrity in their childhood.

I have long puzzled over this curious connection between imitation and freedom. In many ways it is counterintuitive. One would normally think that, if you want a child to be able to exercise freedom as an adult, the best possible preparation would be to give a child many choices and encourage the child to act freely from an early age. Yet such conventional thinking neglects the reality of soul transformation. Material things stay pretty much the same. My chair becomes somewhat worn, the truck acquires some scratches, and my favorite slippers gradually get more comfy, but these things remain recognizable and do not change drastically throughout their useful lifetime. The soul, however, is different. The power of imitation in a young child changes and grows more inward, less visible in outer activity. But the integrity of a child's imitative unity with the environment is slowly transformed into inner integrity, whereby one is united with all parts of one's inner being. There is a connection between appropriate imitation and inner integrity that grounds the individual in self-confidence. An an adult, one is independent, but not during childhood. A child's oneness with the environment is replaced by the adult's unity in Self, which no longer needs to be imposed from outside.

If children are given the opportunity to imitate actions of integrity, then gradually those actions will give the child confidence and security that blossoms as ethical character traits in adulthood. Our actions come from inner strength instead of peer pressure. Thus, if we want to live in a society in which adults can interrelate in the freedom of integrity, we need to attend to the natural imitative inclinations of young children. And, if this freedom of integrity could be exercised in the sense described here, decisions in American boardrooms would have a different character. Ethics depends on the exercise of independent thought.

Now let's turn to the notion of authority. As Steiner says, "Authority develops the rights life." The "rights life" is the social realm in which people relate to one another as equals in the political and social spheres: equal rights, equal pay, equal housing, equal access, and so on. Authority is even less well regarded than imitation. After all, who wants to be bossed around? Are not those in positions of authority often on an ego trip? What about equality? Does authority have any place in a democracy?

It is necessary first to reexamine and redefine our concept of authority. Most people see authority in terms of a position—the President, for example. Along with that comes a host of expectations and assumptions. For our purposes, I would like to describe a new approach to authority, one that is relational.

Imagine being in a modern art museum and encountering a few paintings that take your breath away. You go from one to the other and find that they speak to you in a special way. Of course, you try to find out something about the painter, but the little plaques on the wall give only scanty information. So you drink in the paintings, and for a long time afterward they stay with you as images. Perhaps you return to the museum in later years just to see the pictures again. Or maybe you inquire about that artist at other museums when you travel. Because of your continuing interest and actions, you have developed a relationship with this particular artist.

Many years go by, and one day you are invited to a social gathering, and the host happens to mention that the painter will be there; you catch your breath and eagerly accept the invitation. Now imagine the days, hours, and even the few minutes leading up to the moment when you will finally meet the famous painter. What is going on inside? Anticipation, yes. But there is more. You have developed a feeling that surpasses respect. It is veneration. Anyone who could paint such masterpieces must be an amazing person. You prepare yourself for any encounter, perhaps warning yourself that the person might be wizened and ugly, even hunchbacked. You can accept anything, because you know the soul of that artist through the paintings.

In the minutes before the meeting, you feel like a small child, vulnerable, hopeful, and eager. You may be nervous, but you would not miss the meeting for anything. The actual moment of introduction is a high point in your life story, one that will remain with you forever.

This description would not be complete without the last step: the will to act because of an encounter with a revered artist. In this instance, it might be the decision to enroll in classes with the master, or to offer help in editing a book of the artist's work. This illustration is meant to awaken in adults some feeling for what a child might more readily experience when brought into contact with appropriate authority, especially in the years between ages seven and fourteen:

> All education in this period of life will have to be consciously directed toward awakening in a child a pure, beautiful feeling for authority; for what is to be implanted in the child during these years is to form the foundation for what the adult is to experience in the social organism as the equal human rights. (*ibid.*, p. 14)

When a child experiences reverence for authority and for people worthy of trust, the soul gradually transforms, leading to a social reality in the form of real support for equality. In a sense, authority matures into equal rights in society. For example, when people listen to the music of a great artist, they are filled with reverence. This, in turn, develops respect and empathy. When we are knowledgeable about all aspects of our society and community, we can empathize with people, and this brings about respect for others. Bigotry and fear arise from ignorance of other peoples' lives. A child who is given a structured, nurturing life will develop respect for appropriate authority, which gradually matures into self-respect and respect for others.

According to this way of thinking, the reverse is also true. If a child is given too many choices and is asked to form judgments too early, then a disconnection arises that will lead to antisocial tendencies later in life. Precocious judgments and criticism in childhood can lead to a dog-eat-dog attitude toward others later on. In their drive for personal gain, many push the competition off the ladder, even if it causes hardship for others. There are those who lament the competitive nature of the workplace and the inequity in pay, but few look to the early classroom to intervene. As a cautionary reminder of where this can lead us, consider a popular bumper sticker from a few years ago: "He who dies with the most toys wins." Teachers and parents who treat children like little adults should at least consider the possibility that authority, when properly exercised, could help develop social skills later in life.

And now consider compassion, or "brotherliness, love, develops the economic life," as Steiner says. How in the world can this be related to economics? My father, Siegfried E. Finser, worked for many years in corporate America, for companies such as Xerox and ITT. He also co-founded the Rudolf Steiner Foundation, a nonprofit organization that provides alternative funding solutions for schools, clinics, businesses, farms, and community projects all over North America. When asked about how compassion in a child leads to a healthy sense for economic life in the adult, he responded:

> I know it only from the other way around. If we look into the ideals of economic life, we find at its roots the fostering of brotherhood. Any business that is focused fully on meeting the needs of humanity through the needs of the customer learns quickly the right relationship. It will prosper as long as it serves a need. Regardless of how marketing tries to create or make people aware of needs they didn't know they had, this principle still holds true. (from a personal conversation)

He noted that there are many stories of how a business starts out with one goal in mind, but that customers want something else, and so gradually the business must swing around to meet their needs. The Harlemville Farm Store is a prime example. It began as an outlet for the farm's products. One hundred percent of the items for sale there came from the Harlemville farm dairy, its yogurt production and the gardens. Customers shopped there for that reason. However, the customers asked for other products they needed: bread, cheese, butter, baked goods, and then teas, dried fruits, jams, and so on. The farm could not keep up with the needs of its customers, so the store began to buy from other wholesalers to satisfy their customers. Today, less than two percent of the stores sales comes from the farm. It is a most successful operation, because it was forced to meet the needs of its customers.

In fact, every sales transaction is a social act that has at its roots a longing to meet the physical and earthly needs of humanity. My father believes that, as time continues into future stages of our society's evolution, we will see brotherhood unfold from the present economic situation.

He continued to talk about the division of labor—its history, when it entered society, and how it leads to specialization, which in turn demands that we depend on each other more than ever before. Workers on an assembly line depend on the preceeding workers on the line doing their jobs properly, and they each make it possible through their own work for the next in line to do their jobs properly. This was not true of a shoemaker, who made the entire shoe. Shoemakers could claim credit for the complete product. Workers today might be able say only that they helped make a car by installing the rear window.

My father went on to say that we have seen the local village economy evolve into a division of labor, moving from currency and barter to credit and the specialization of professions. No manufactured product exists today, except by virtue of this world economy. Take apart any manufactured appliance or machine—a refrigerator or a car—and you will discover the interdependence of the economy as a whole. The parts all came from different places in the world, and this required a communications, distribution, and transportation systems, and a financial system that makes possible the rapid transfer of capital and payments. It is a system that relies on cooperation, and in the current economic crises we can see that, when our leaders fail to make ethical decisions, the economy suffers. Therefore, the logical development is a world economy based on cooperation and an intention toward the well-being and health of all.

After considering imitation, authority, and compassion, one might well ask: What if I lived through a childhood without these experiences? Am I doomed to fail as an ethical individual? Of course not. But the process given to children as a natural potential must be cultivated in adults through conscious self-development. We can work on ourselves to "catch up" with what we missed as children. Even if we fail sometimes, the effort itself helps start a sequence of soul awakenings that can help solve the ethical dilemma of our time. A good way to address this as adults is by conscious self-development.

By "conscious self-development" I mean an honest self-appraisal that can lead to self-initiated remediation or change. For example, when reviewing your own childhood, you might find that, based on accounts from family members, there was considerable imitation and a certain amount of compassion, but the experience of appropriate authority was missing. If reflection determines that this was indeed the case, it is possible to be especially awake as an adult to situations in which equality comes into play. By developing listening skills, for example—by walking in the shoes of another—one can stand on the same ground as the other adults one meets in the workplace. Recently a parent said, "My child's teacher answered my question but never acknowledged the turmoil we have been through." She was looking for empathy as well as an answer, because empathy is one of the most valuable social assets we have at our disposal these days. This equation, however, is not just about one person; society in general needs to learn a healthy respect for authority. We can all do things in the countless small moments of the day to cultivate this respect. As J. K. Rowling's character Dumbledore says in *The Chamber of Secrets,* it is not the talents that we bring, but the many choices we make that matter most. Every adult moment in life is a choice, and the ways we meet those countless choices determines the world we live in, every bit as much as it does the quality of our childhood.

MATERIALISM

In J. R. R. Tolkein's *Hobbit*, countless readers have encountered the unusual character of Gollum. Slimy, insidious, and crafty, he is first encountered deep beneath the earth, where he lives on an island in the middle of a lake. Gollum's prized possession is his magic ring, which he inadvertently looses to the Hobbit Bilbo. For the rest of his miserable life, Gollum searches for his "precious"—the ring that can make one invisible. Only at the very end of the epic story does he reclaim it as he falls over the precipice into the raging fires below. Gollum and his ring perish together.

Each time I have encountered Gollum when reading Tolkein's stories to my children, I am struck by the theme of "possession." This curious figure is so obsessed with his lost possession that it in fact possesses him. He walks miles, endures hunger and cold and all sorts of deprivation for the sake of the ring, which truly has hold of him. Gollum's life is filled with desire, and the desire rules his life.

Of course, the ring is extraordinary. It has an allure that can tempt anyone, but especially those who have worn it for a time. Tolkein's ring aptly illustrates the incredible fascination that men and women today have with possessions. Lives are spent in the pursuit of wealth, and although we do not look like Gollum outwardly, the soul configuration is often shockingly similar. There are people who will sacrifice everything for material success, including quality time with their children, marriages, and even personal health. We all know people who are obsessed with acquiring things. Consider Martha Stuart. If we can believe what we read, there are many examples of how Martha used friends for her own gain. One person was enlisted to help with a video production and promised a fifty-percent contract but, after much of the work was completed, was handed a contract that gave her only ten percent. Most likely, this is only one example and just the tip of the proverbial iceberg.

Materialism has a grip on humanity as never before. I have concluded that it is a form of addiction and should be treated as such. People buy even when they need nothing. Shopping is a pastime, a form of entertainment, and a quick fix. Look at the symptoms: mailboxes filled with catalogues; glassy-eyed, mindless teenagers roaming the malls; cars traded in after only a couple of years, just because the owner became bored with the old one; and clothes, purchased and worn once or twice before being discarded.

In the fall of 2002, I spent a few days in Katmandu and experienced a very different situation. Unpaved city streets lined with shacks, children playing with bits of wood and stones, fathers and mothers trying to sell a few trinkets in their hole-in-the-wall stores, and the aged cast from their homes, wandering the streets. I visited a clinic for leprosy patients, heard the stories of abuse, and met the children picked up off the street, some of whom had been serving as slaves. Foods such as eggs and fresh meat were sold in the open marketplace with no refrigeration, the schools were in the final stages of disintegration, and the government was divided up into feuding factions, with the result that there were essentially no social services.

In the face of all this poverty, I was doubly impressed with the joyful celebrations at the Tihar festival. At night, candles lined the windowsills and pathways of dwellings, people gathered for song and celebration, and community was visible. These people who had so little were rich in other ways. They were grateful for the clothes we brought from home for their children. I was greeted everywhere with joy and respect, a nod of the head and hands pressed together in blessing.

As I returned home from Nepal, my sense was that we live in a divided world. Not just the simplistic divisions of rich and poor, east and west, but also a division of focus. In a place so full of poverty, I found abundant spirituality and culture. And here, where there is so much affluence, I find constant dissatisfaction and hollow thrills. I returned to this affluence with my own mailbox overflowing with catalogues, while the children of Nepal and many other places long for a book with pictures.

The instances of leprosy in Nepal made a profound impression on me, so much so that it is still difficult to articulate. But it was clear that the illnesses and homelessness of so many children and elderly people were the results of poverty that had gone on too long. And what are the consequences of our materialism, our affluence? Whereas the consequences of leprosy are visible in outer extremity of skin and missing fingers, toes, and feet, the consequences of materialism are masked. In Western cultures, we use the majority of the world's resources, and we expect comforts and a lifestyle that would be impossible if it were not for people elsewhere laboring at very low wages. We pride ourselves on having abolished slavery, yet a form of economic servitude remains that is equally harsh for those in the world's sweatshops. I have often thought that, just as we have warnings from the Surgeon General on cigarettes, we should also have labels on products made in factories that use child labor. After years of exploitation, people become angry, and violence can result. Terrorism is a form of anger, and as much as I disagree with those who commit violence, I do not feel we can continue to tolerate conditions that produce the "grapes of wrath" around the world.

With increasing frequency, the masks of materialism are lifted for the public to see, and we are shocked. The inner activity—the minds and hearts—of many of our politicians, business leaders, and priests has become corrupted, and occasionally they are exposed. Whether it is a politician receiving illegal campaign contributions or gifts, a business executive doing phony energy trades, or a priest abusing children, they are all fixated on the physical. Materialism wants to make us slaves to our lower selves.

The issue of ethics cannot be solved by introducing new and better courses in leadership ethics; it must be addressed by a total renewal of our social ideals. Until we can lift our eyes above the ground and see the sun, moon, and stars of the spiritual world, we will continue to grovel like so many Gollums searching for the magic ring.

FORMING JUDGMENTS

In reflecting on the story of Kenneth Lay and others who once led major corporations such as Enron, I am disturbed by the capacity of such supposedly able and intelligent men to make such poor decisions. What were they thinking? Were they living in such a bubble that they thought no one would ever find out? How could they make such bad judgments?

Media coverage of ethical issues in business has involved much hand wringing and lamentation over the abuses of power we've seen in recent years. The media has moved from one story to another in a sanguine, superficial manner. Deep down, however, many carry around unanswered questions that sit in the soul like so many rocks. I have spoken with very few people who feel that their need to understand the deeper questions will be satisfied by labeling certain CEOs as "bad guys" and then waiting years for the justice system to run its course. What seems to be multiple and diverse voices in the media are really just one, because all may be owned by a parent corporation and allowed to feed upon one another. A movie made by one company under a parent company will be featured in a "news" program by another company that is part of the same corporate conglomerate. Much of this is self-serving and designed to boost the bottom line of ratings and sponsors.

Nevertheless, not all corporate executives are evil, and many—not just those in business—may feel that the transgressions of some are human failings that could tempt any one of us. Can we dig deeper to understand these faulty judgments, so that we can learn from them? One possible path of inquiry is that of understanding consciousness. Put simply, we all experience times of sleeping, dreaming, and being fully awake. The boundaries between these states of consciousness are not as finite as commonly believed. For example, even during the day, while working or playing, there are moments when one might dream for a short while, or even slip into a short sleep. We often return from these moments with a different perspective, a different feeling or resolution. This is because dreams involve feelings, and sleep can stir the will to action.

Based on the psychology of the soul that I have studied and worked with, known as Anthroposophy, there is a profound difference in the three states of consciousness just mentioned. They affect our ability to form conclusions, judgments, and concepts:

> Conclusions can live and be healthy only in the living human spirit. That is, the conclusion is healthy only when it exists in completely conscious life.... Conclusions should never trickle down into the dreaming soul, only judgments. But everything we make in the way of judgments about the world trickles down into the dreaming soul. What is this dreaming soul, really? As we have learned, it is more feeling-oriented. When we form a judgment and then go on with our lives, we carry our judgments with us through the world. However, we carry them in the feeling, and that means judging is a kind of habit [and] what we develop as concepts descends into the deepest depths of human nature and, considered spiritually, descends into the sleeping soul.... Concepts can live in the unconscious. Judgments can live only as habits in semiconscious dreaming, and conclusions should actually be present only in the fully conscious waking life.[3]

All of this has, of course, profound implications as to how we teach children, but for the purposes of ethical leadership, I want to particularly focus on the habit-forming qualities of judgment.

---

3. Rudolf Steiner, *The Foundations of Human Experience*, pp. 150–153.

According to Egyptian mythology, at death a person is judged by Osiris and his assisting judges, who determine what sins that person has committed. The individual's heart is placed on one side of a scale, and on the other side a feather that represents truth. If the heart is as light as a feather, the soul is allowed to proceed. We still use the expression "I feel as light as a feather," indicating the buoyancy that arises when we have few worldly cares. This is a good state for us, especially before death. The central image of the Egyptian teaching is a scale. It was used to measure, assess, and determine the fate of a person's soul. One often sees people use the right and left hands and arms in a scale-like gesture. With arms outstretched, we express our feelings, judging what we encounter in life. Our breathing, even our heartbeat, changes with the various feelings we experience. As with the respiratory and the circulatory system, movement is essential, and blockages can even lead to a fatal illness. In working with the realm of judging and feeling and dreaming, therefore, we need to look to flow and movement. The old-fashioned scales show vividly how movement, from left to right, or down and up, will eventually come to rest, and there is the moment of judgment. When I need to wrestle with something, when I sense a dilemma in life, I often go for a walk. Even with small things, like writer's block, a few minutes outside in the fresh air and in movement will get me going again.

Many schoolchildren today are fed a mental diet of finished conclusions and fixed concepts. They are given abstract theories and finite definitions, which are then retrieved, or not, in tests. The weighing processes of judgment formation are short-changed. John Holt, the author of *How Children Fail*, says that children become information junkies and learn to please the teachers by regurgitating what has been taught. The middle realm of heart and lung—of processing and judging—is gradually bypassed, and the soul becomes cramped.

Instead, children deserve living concepts: ideas that can change with time, characterizations from different points of view, and artistic experiences that enhance the ability to judge. In the creative aspects of learning, when a child becomes Hiawatha in a dramatic production, there is a living, maturing process at work. Children need to become what they learn, not just ingest it. A painting or drawing allows colors to be absorbed in in a way that works on a child's feelings, as does a circle song or dance. Our schools need to provide children with more opportunities to work with life-giving arts, and fewer deadening conclusions and concepts. In an ideal world, a child would be allowed to experience a subject, gradually awaken to the conclusions inherent in the lesson, and form concepts that might not blossom for years. The best lessons come with time.

So, how does all this affect ethical leadership? In addition to the whole area of mis-education and the subsequent challenges today, we can look specifically at the judgments of our leaders. Rather than an atmosphere of open, healthy exchange with stockholders and others, rather than an inner process of weighing and characterizing, these leaders were trapped in a cage. Of course, from between the bars, they had a limited view of the public and their clients. But essentially, these modern executives were trapped in a cage of finite possibilities. The bars of the cage represented accountants, lawyers, and others who gave the advice they thought the CEO, wanted to hear. These advisors were caught in the world of their personal limitations. Their work habits and ways of forming judgments were too narrow for moral, ethical considerations.

One way we can renew our ability to form judgments and to discern is through artistic and creative practice. In drawing, for example, we perceive the colors, judge what needs to come next, and introduce new forms and shades based on our judgment of the whole. This is ongoing when drawing or painting, and builds inner flexibility in our ability to make judgments.

DESIRE

In regard to modern ethics, desire is recognized as greed; it has been an issue from the earliest times. Buddhism describes an eightfold path designed to overcome desire and the thirst for things through a sequence of exercises that, if practiced, can bring objectivity and enlightenment. Rudolf Steiner discussed this Eightfold Path in *According to Luke:*

> In the eightfold path, [the Buddha] wanted to show humankind the route to knowledge uninfluenced by *samskara*.[4] He said that we achieve this type of knowledge by acquiring right views that have nothing to do with sympathy, antipathy, or personal bias. We develop such views purely on the basis of what is presented to us from outside, that is, on the basis of the object's own forces. "Right views," or "right understanding" of issues, is the first step on the eightfold path.
>
> As a second step, we must become independent of persistent remnants of previous incarnations. We must attempt to form judgments based on right views rather than on any other influences. "Right judgment" is the second step.
>
> The third is to express our right views and right judgments correctly when we convey them to the world. We refrain from introducing anything other than our right views into our words and any other expressions of our human nature. This is the "right speech" of Buddhism.
>
> The fourth necessary step is to carry out actions uninfluenced by our sympathies and antipathies, free of the dark rumblings of samskara. We permit only our right views, right judgment, and right speech to affect our deeds. This is "right action."

---

4. *Samskara* (Sanskrit), literally, to improve, refine, impress. In Hindu philosophy, it refers to impressions left on the mind by actions or outer circumstances and capable of being developed. *Samskara* is the seeds of propensities and impulses from previous births to be developed in this or future incarnations.

The fifth step toward inner liberation is achieving our proper place in the world. What did the Buddha mean by this? Many people are unsatisfied with their task in the world and think they would be better off in a different position. We need to learn, however, to make the best of the situation that is ours through birth or destiny. When we are not content with our station in life, it does not provide the strength we need for appropriate action in the world. The Buddha called this fifth step acquiring the "right standpoint."

The sixth step is to make a habit of everything we have acquired through right views, right judgment, and so forth. Already as children, we begin to develop specific habits and inclinations. We must make an effort, however, to give up habits that come from *samskara* and to gradually acquire ones that result from right views, right judgment, right speech, and so forth. These are "right habits."

The seventh step is to order our life by not forgetting yesterday when we act today. If we had to learn all our skills anew each time we attempted to do something, we would never accomplish anything. We must always attempt to recollect or remember all aspects of our existence, to evaluate what we have already learned and link the present to the past. This "right memory" must be acquired on the eightfold path of Buddhism.

The eighth step is accomplished by allowing neither our preference for a specific opinion nor anything that persists from previous incarnations to interfere with the purity of our contemplation of the objects and events we encounter. We allow the objects and events themselves to speak for themselves. This is "right contemplation." (pp. 72–74)

The objectivity that arises even from the early stages of work on this path tends to lessen the influence of passing judgments and to direct attention away from opinion to truthfulness based upon reality. Rather than creating "truths" that live in half realities (read balance sheets, stockholder reports), the Eightfold

Path encourages the objectivity that comes from clear vision of what is actually there, what is grounded in reality. Secondly, the person who works on this path of purification will gradually overcome the desires that usually beset us, including the desire for money and worldly success.

SELF-INTEREST

All of modern culture, right into the spiritual areas, is based upon human self-interest.... Due to this self-centeredness, people want to continue to exist when they go through the gates of death: they want to retain their I. Although very refined, this is one form of egoism.[5]

Steiner goes on to say that the emphasis on death instead of also considering birth perpetuates the self-interest of humanity that has lead to immorality. Nakota Elder Grandmother Kitty referred to this as "survival mode." She used to say that you can always trust people to do what they need to do for their own survival.

During the 1990s, many involved in technology and start-up companies made a whole lot of money. What was particularly interesting was the way their compensation was structured. Relatively modest amounts were paid directly as salary, but potentially very valuable stock options were granted. For the companies that succeeded, these options created millionaires. This was seen as a reward for innovation and risk taking. Yet, unlike a salary, which has some relation to the work done, options created a whole new class based on employees "cashing in" on rising stock prices. So the value of a company's stock became a huge focus for those in leadership positions.

What is a stock? It is a purchased share in a company and traded publicly on a stock exchange. Traditionally, the value of stocks has risen or fallen according to the company's earnings

---

5. Rudolf Steiner, *The Foundations of Human Experience*, p. 36.

and performance. One rather simple perspective describes stock as a share of the public's confidence in a company. When there is a lot of confidence in a company's management, fundamental cash flow, and return on equity, the public tends to value its stock more highly. Stock is supposed to represent economic reality. Unfortunately, some executives began to manipulate the public's perception of company earnings and performance and, thereby, artificially inflated the prices of their stock. Accounting procedures were adjusted, transactions were misrepresented, and financial reports became a tangle of half-truths. The public was deceived for the benefit of a few, who could thus increase their personal wealth.

Besides these basics of greed, what is this self-interest all about? Self-awareness and consideration of one's needs are required for a healthy life. If we continually expend energy and never replenish, for example, we burn out.[6] It is important to recognize the symptoms of burnout and to take steps to heal oneself. We all need time to reflect, take time off, and change activities to balance our daily demands. Yet, in our modern world, there seem to be two extremes: to merge with the needs of others so much that we lose ourselves, on the one hand, and, on the other, to harden ourselves into self-centered egoists.

Either extreme has its perils. Merging with the needs of others leads to personal problems, because it usually manifests within families. Women, usually the family caregivers, become immersed in the day-to-day needs of husband, children, elderly parents, and even siblings, and, as a result, the well-being of the whole family can suffer. Even in the workplace, merging with the needs of others causes problems, because the work environment absorbs whatever energy is put into it. Of these two extremes, hardening into self seems to bring the greatest challenges for many in public life today. Politicians think more about reelection than public service, and many business leaders think

---

6. I discuss the issue of burnout in my book *School Renewal*.

more about net worth and stock prices than public good. Even the word service has become almost synonymous with "marketing" rather than doing something positive for the community.

The topics discussed in this chapter are related to ethics: the social issues of materialism, desire, self-interest, and forming false judgments of one another. We cannot expect our leaders to uphold ideas that we ourselves cannot affirm. The social fabric influences the quality of the leaders that emerge. We need to work toward a general awakening; the way you treat the world is the way the world will treat you. And with that conscious intention, every single person can begin to work for change.

4. Historical Considerations

ETHICAL LEADERSHIP

Read a newspaper or watch a show on TV, then stop and reflect on what you have taken in. How much of it is true? How much can you substantiate? Every day we take in countless bits of information, and, unfortunately, much of it is interpretation, inaccurate, or worse, untruthful. We live in the age of the lie. Everywhere we have shading of the truth and a tendency to obscure the facts. Why is this? In part, our thirst for material comfort has led us down the path of untruth. We seem to have so many needs, and the more we acquire, the more we seem to need, and so we work even harder. In striving for more, some become so tempted by material possessions that they do almost anything to get what they want. One means—manipulation—is rampant today, from innocently sharing selective information to outright dishonesty. Behind all this is the voracious monster we call greed, and along the way, truth gets trampled.

Recent events in business have made us aware of this more than ever. Top executives at Enron, WorldCom, ImClone and other companies have manipulated revenue reports and mis-represented earnings. Once they are sliding down that slippery slope, it becomes harder and harder for companies to reverse course. Now executives of these companies are facing jail time. The addiction we call materialism leads us to question the actions of our leaders more than ever before. Unlike times in the past, when leadership was often synonymous with moral-ity, we now find unethical political and business leaders. We hear of religious leaders accused of molesting children. Together, the church, business, and political dissolution is a far greater crisis than many realize. We are suffering from serious moral decay.

For many leaders today, ethics is discovered in the marketplace of business or politics, not in the sanctum of self-reflection. Our culture seems to provide little guidance in regard to ethics, and the "inner compass" seems not to be functioning. It's as if a veil is blocking the truth. The focus of most leaders seems to be obscured, having shifted toward the bottom line. Leaders caught in one transgression or another often seem surprised, as if they thought they would get away with it or simply had no clue about where they had gone astray.

In order to examine the historical aspect of ethical leadership, let us consider the best known of the early Greek philosophers. Then we will examine other thinkers down through the ages who have contributed to the ongoing discussion of ethics.

Whereas Plato "believed in the existence of an absolute standard to which human conduct must be referred and by which its ethical quality must be measured," Aristotle is concerned "with the practice rather than the theory of morals. To become a good man you must behave like a good man. Then you will know what goodness is. Ethics is the science, or if you like, the art, of making that discovery."[1] Just as in classroom management, teachers set standards or expectations of ethical behavior, they also judge compliance of such by the observable behavior of the children. So the issue in public life is a matter of either finding a common ground for ethical standards (as in Plato's ideals), or simply judging our leaders according to their behavior (as Aristotle would have us do).

In the classic debate on ethics between Plato and Aristotle, there are aspects of each viewpoint that are appealing. Plato's assertion that there is an absolute standard makes sense, since

---

1.   Johnathan Barnes, introduction to *The Ethics of Aristotle,* p. 23.

one is either lying or not; one has either broken a law or not. Society needs clear, unambiguous standards, so that people can orient themselves accordingly. On an ordinary level, one might say, "Did I really come to a complete halt at that stop sign, or was I just going more slowly?" We would like to make everything relative: "I slowed down, therefore I was stopping." In fact, *stop* means "stop." What is the inner equivalent of a stop sign? According to Plato, it would be the values we carry: truth, beauty, and virtue—ideals that can be just as real as a street sign. If these ideals are present, they can guide our actions; we need only to consult our inner compass to know right from wrong.

Aristotle was oriented much more toward the world of the senses; he saw actions and lifestyles as the manifestation of ethical practice: "The manner of a man in life is a clue to what he, on reflection, regards as the good" (*ibid.*, p. 30). This raises some interesting possibilities when looking for ethics in the workplace. What is it about the "manner of a man in life" that can support ethical behavior in the workplace?

One means of addressing the manner of a person's life would be for organizations to devote time and resources to discussing life skills that support ethics in the workplace. These conversations might focus on key questions such as those posed by business author Joseph J. Badaracco, Jr., in his article "Discipline of Building Character." He articulates the importance of defining moments when leaders must act out of deeply rooted values. The way we perform in these crucial moments can set the course of conduct in an organization for years to come. Do we base our work on ethical "myopia" or on some degree of self-reflection and awareness? To facilitate the latter, Badaracco encourages dialogue and reflection on the individual, group, and corporate level around certain key questions (Badaracco, pp. 112–113):

For Individuals

Who am I?

1. What feelings and intuitions are coming into conflict in this situation?

2. Which of the values that are in conflict are most deeply rooted in my life?

3. What combination of expediency and shrewdness, coupled with imagination and boldness, will help me implement my personal understanding of what is right?

For Managers of Work Groups

Who are we?

1. What are the other strong, persuasive interpretations of the ethics of this situation?

2. What point of view is most likely to win a contest of interpretations inside my organization and influence the thinking of other people?

3. Have I orchestrated a process that can make manifest the values I care about in my organization? (*ibid.*)

Using these as starting points, leaders can model self-reflection, followed by "review meetings" in which members of a group are able to describe situations that involve competing values, and the group can engage in conversation. Case studies can be presented. This method places ethical considerations on the table and heightens awareness of the many large and small dilemmas that we all face each day. Members of groups would then be more inclined to check in with each other on an individual basis, for shared perspective can enhance the soul breadth that is needed for value-based workplaces.

> As for the life of the businessman, it does not give him much freedom of action. Besides, wealth is obviously not the good we seek, for the sole purpose it serves is to provide the means of getting something else (Aristotle, p. 31).

Aristotle made the point hundreds of years ago that wealth is not an end in itself, but only a means to support a more contemplative life. Danger arises when wealth is seen as good in itself. After distinguishing three kinds of "good"—that of outer world, that of the soul, and that of the body—Aristotle says, "the goods of the soul are the best and are most properly designated as 'good'" (*ibid.*, p. 41). In the Olympics, the awards do not go to those who look good, but to those who compete successfully; likewise, in ethics, it is our actions that count most. One is a "no good man who does not find pleasure in noble deeds" (*ibid.*, p. 42). One definition of *noble* is "refined," something no longer coarse or vulgar. To be refined is to be aware of the surrounding world and how we affect that world. All noble deeds come from this kind of sensibility, and they are our good actions in the world. But what guides our actions?

CONSCIENCE

Conscience is more than just the ability to say "this is good" or "that is bad," or to know what to do or not do. Rudolf Steiner noted that the medieval mystic Meister Eckhart "tells of a tiny spark that underlies conscience; an eternal element in the soul which, if it is heeded, declares with unmistakable power the laws of good and evil."[2] And the German philosopher Johann Gottlieb Fichte

> held that the highest experience for the human ego was the experience of conscience, when man hears the inward judgment: "This you must do, for it would go against your conscience not to do it."... He ranked conscience as the ego's most significant impulse. (*ibid.*, p. 103)

All of us have experienced that moment of discomfort in which we hear the inward judgment. It may be in a moment of thoughtless gossip or in a moment of deliberate untruth.

---

2. Rudolf Steiner, *Metamorphoses of the Soul*, vol. 2, p. 102.

The further we move on into modern times, and the more our thinking becomes materialistic, the more do we find conscience deprived of its majesty—not in the human heart, but in the thinking of philosophers who are more or less imbued with materialism. (*ibid.*, p. 103)

Nowadays people often see conscience as the sum of habits and judgments instilled during the early years and strengthened by life experience. Conscience is seen as conditioned by the environment. A contemporary example can be found in the movie *Trading Places*. Two old buddies, both commodities traders, make a bet. One asserts that character, conscience, and goodness are hereditary; these qualities are either present or not. The other believes that such qualities are the result of environmental influences. They pick two individuals: a young executive of their firm and a homeless man on the street. They engineer events so that the two end up trading places unwillingly. In the end, the environment argument prevails, but with a few humorous twists, so that the jaded commodities traders get their just desserts.

Both Socrates and Plato believed that virtue can be learned and acquired. Knowledge of virtue can help a person learn to act virtuously. In Steiner's view, the inner voice of conscience can speak long before we learn to tell good from bad. Children can act out of compassion and fairness long before they have formed concepts about those qualities. So how do we strengthen this inner voice in the souls of our children?

According to Steiner, the ego is less active in the sentient soul (passions, desires, likes versus dislikes); somewhat more active in the intellectual soul (as one reflects on experience); and most active in the consciousness soul. In what Steiner refers to as our consciousness soul, as the ego, or I, develops, it becomes increasingly radiant until, eventually, it lives with full clarity and awareness. At this point of clarity, we have matured and taken hold of ourselves and our goals, which we have made intentional. If we agree with Fichte—that conscience is the highest experience for the human ego—conscience is the pearl, won through hard labor, from the shell of our existence. "Cleaning out," or spiritual work, is essential to transformation.

In the past, good and evil were experienced as pictures or images from outside oneself, as seen in many myths and fairy tales (dragons, princes, and so on). These stories and myths provide the symbols of good and evil. Over time, these were gradually replaced by the inner voice of conscience that can be found in the center of the soul. That which was once experienced externally is now mirrored in the human soul. External vision becomes inward experience.

Consider Greek drama as an example of the shift from external symbols to inner dialogue. *Oresteia*, by Aeschylus, begins with the play *Agamemnon*. Agamemnon, the triumphant leader of the Greek forces in Troy, returns home to Argos after abducting Cassandra, the prophet of Apollo and daughter of Priam, the defeated ruler of Troy. Upon Agamemnon's return, his wife Clytaemnestra murders him in revenge for sacrificing their daughter Iphigeneia and for the insult of Cassandra's presence. Clytaemnestra then places herself and her lover Aegisthus on the throne of Argos. The second play, *The Libation Bearers*, deals with the actions of the children of Agamemnon—Electra and Orestes—as they mourn their father. Electra urges Orestes to avenge their father's death by killing their mother Clytaemnestra, even though this means committing matricide. Orestes travels to Delphi and asks the Oracle whether he should avenge his father's murder. Apollo appears and tells him that, if he does not avenge his father's death, he will be cast from society. Orestes obeys Apollo, returns to Argos and murders his mother and Aegisthus. What, then, is the consequence for Orestes?

Through the visionary dreams of both Clytaemnestra and Orestes, the playwright reveals how the heinous crime of matricide evokes a mode of seeing that was no longer common. The enormity of the crime caused the old clairvoyance, or visions, to awaken as an inheritance from the past. Clytaemnestra had a dream about giving birth to a snake, but when she swaddled it and brought it to her breast, it struck her. After the murder of his mother, Orestes tells the chorus that, even though he has been told by Apollo to commit these acts, he "must escape this blood ... it is my own." It is then that he sees the approach of the Erinyes—or furies, as they were later called by the Romans (*ibid.*, p. 111). No one else can see these women, who look like Gorgons, shrouded in black, their heads wreathed with swarming serpents. Thus, in the second play of the Oresteian trilogy, we are given a powerful picture of how the old clairvoyance awakens in Orestes.

The Erinyes are the old forces of earth. They come forth to avenge matricide, because they are responsible for infringement of sacred blood ties. The death of Agammenon was preceded by the atrocities of his grandfather Tantalus, who feasted on his son Pelops' flesh, and when Pelops is restored to life, he murders Hippodameia's father in a ruse for her hand. Their two sons, Atreus and Thyestes, compete for the throne. Atreus lures Thyestes to a feast and feeds him the flesh of his own children, whereby Thyestes curses the house of Atreus. Aegisthus, Thyestes' son, and Agamemnon, Atreus' son, continue the blood feud in *Oresteia*. It is a history of bloodshed and revenge from generation to generation. Now Orestes has committed matricide, and this action invokes the feminine forces of the earth.

In dreamlike clairvoyance, Orestes sees the outer effect of his act of matricide—the Erinyes. Apollo has approved his action, but something higher must be appeased. In the last play, *The Eumenides*, the playwright Aeschylus indicates that there is an even higher cosmic ordinance, which he could comply with only by making Orestes clairvoyant at that moment, because he had not yet gone far enough to dramatize what we call an "inner voice" today. When we study his work, we feel that he was at the stage where something like conscience ought to emerge from the whole content of the human soul, but he never quite reaches that point. He confronts Orestes with dreamlike, clairvoyant pictures of the Furies, which have not yet been transformed into conscience. Through the visions of Erinyes, which hound Orestes to the ends of the earth, we see how Aeschylus is on the verge of recognizing conscience. Every word that the playwright gives Clytaemnestra, for example, makes one feel unmistakably that he ought to indicate the idea of conscience in its present-day sense; but he never quite gets that far. In that century, the great poet could show only how malevolent actions arose before the human soul in earlier times.

By the end of the last play of this trilogy, Apollo, Orestes, and the Erinyes bring their case to the goddess Athena. She presents a new solution from Zeus, who authorizes a jury of Athenian citizens. When the votes are cast, it is a tie for condemnation and acquittal. It is Athena, symbolizing the intellect and wisdom, who makes the final decision for mercy. She offers to appease the furies by giving them an abode deep in the earth below Athens and the power to punish all violence—not just that of the bloodlines, but also of the state and polis. Athena's words tell us that, despite Orestes' acquittal, he still carries the guilt of his act. Thus, in a kind of archetypal act of ethical individualism, she replaces the act of revenge with the act of atonement.

When we turn to the plays of Euripides, however, we see that although only one generation has passed, there is a significant change in what is portrayed. Now the dreamlike pictures that Orestes experienced are no more than shadowy images of the inner stirring of conscience. We also see this in a variety of Shakespearean plays, from *Hamlet* to *Macbeth*. The characters continually question their actions whether in supplication to the gods or as aside to their own conscience. What was seen in pictures or images now lives in the soul, even in the tortured soul of a protagonist.

These examples reveal that human beings evolved gradually toward the experience of conscience as an inner reality. God in the natural world of the groves and shrines of our ancestors became moving pictures in dreams, oracular vision, and then became the inward seeing of our conscience. Thus the eighteenth-century philosopher Fichte says that conscience is the highest voice in our inner life. Our very dignity as human beings is inseparable from conscience, and when we fall from that high voice, as through the acts of those Enron executives, we lose more than stock options. All of humanity falls back a step and loses that highest voice through such impaired judgment in ethics.

What does it mean to be a human being? Other forms of life interact, search for means of survival, and propagate. What is it to be human? That part of our nature that is not animal, not plant, and not stone is an inner sanctuary, which some call conscience. According to Steiner, we have ego consciousness, or awareness of self, and our soul embraces the in-dwelling of the sacred Self. Our conscience is our most sacred individual possession; if we ignore it or give it away to outer material desires, we give away our humanity. When we listen to that inner voice, we can find the fullness of life and determine our direction and goals. When conscience speaks, we lead from within and are intrinsically ethical.

Aeschylus, Euripides, Shakespeare, and other great playwrights help us understand that there has been a journey from the universe without to the universe within. In our conscience, we have a powerful drop of the divine. "When conscience speaks in the human soul, God is speaking" (*ibid.*, p. 115).

LEADERSHIP INTUITION

In times long past, the destinies of whole nations were entrusted to purely intuitive insight; and, as history tells us, the ancient world was largely shaped by the words of prophets, seers, sybils and oracles. With the growth of analytical intellect in our own time, we have lost these prophetic gifts; and yet, with a solid foundation of factual knowledge and intellectual reasoning to serve as a safeguard against illusions, our intuitive faculties can still be used to guide our steps. (Winkler, p. 5)

Dr. Franz Winkler published *The Psychology of Leadership* in 1957. Using insights made possible through the new psychology of Anthroposophy, he wrote about the one-sided tendencies of our time and about the danger that human genius may become obsolete. "The free world will find itself entirely without leaders, for the inventive spirit in man is also his genius for leadership." Winkler often speaks of genius and intuition in reference to leadership. What is this special quality?

Returning once again to ancient Greeks, we can see that what was once on the outside as the Furies is now on the inside as a Sybil, or oracle, in the form of our individual conscience. These archetypal symbols of divine intervention, or deus ex machina, are now internalized with respect to ethical behavior. The classical Greek playwright Aeschylus described the Erynnes, or the Furies, as the goddesses of vengeance who followed Orestes as a wrongdoer. Orestes could see them with their frightening heads covered with snakes as coming from the outside. But, just a short while later, dramatic plays began to show the evildoer as nagged from within. Hamlet, the Prince of Denmark, asks himself whether he should "suffer the slings and arrows of outrageous fortune" or "take arms" against them. The Furies of ancient times have become human soul forces. When we become one-sided in modern society, as Winkler states, and focus only on the material aspects of life, we run the risk that we will lose this gift of genius. We must insure the continued development of conscience by becoming aware of this divine gift.

To look at this transition symbolically, let's consider Pegasus, the winged being of ancient Greece. When the hero Perseus faced the Medusa, whose gaze turned men to stone, he used a brightly polished shield given to him by Athena. As he looked into the shield he was able to cut off the Medusa's head. The winged horse Pegasus sprang from the blood of the decapitated

Medusa. It was said that Pegasus was born from the coupling of Medusa and Poseidon of the waters in one of Athena's temples—hence Athena's anger and willingness to assist Perseus in his quest. In fact, the Muses presented Pegasus to Athena, and he is associated with the gift of poetry in particular. As I imagine this marvelous creature, I see a large, white horse with wings that are strong yet almost transparent. He gallops on the earth and leaps into flight with one effortless rush of movement. Above all, it is the wings that take my breath away.

Transparency, as symbolized by the winged horse Pegasus, is a quality that carries us to another world. Similarly, intuition is also full of movement, yet invisible. Like the horse, it is dedicated to serving the rider, in this case the I of the human being. Yet when I think of horses, I also see will in action, and there is an element of will inherent in intuition. The gift of intuition requires a kind of surrender, an emptying and giving oneself to service. This requires strength and the inner discipline of will. When will is used successfully along with self-surrender, one creates a vessel into which energy can stream. This sun-filled influx of energy is intuition.

It is an inner gesture, or indication, that one lives from a state of pure freedom. Intuition is the highest servant of the ego, because it weds us to heaven. It is our only real hope, our own thread of transparency that connects us to the higher worlds. It is a soul force that belongs to the greater good. My description of intuition consciousness is that it is a soul-spiritual gesture that is growing today, but more than anything it belongs to the future. A spiritual gesture is a connection of heaven and earth. The Notebooks of Leonardo Da Vinci contain a famous study of human proportions, showing two images of a man who, in the top image, has his feet on the ground and his arms stretched out to either side. This is superimposed on a second image in which the man appears to have moved his feet farther apart and lifted his arms. This image shows the concept of a spiritual gesture. As human beings, when we experience a natural phenomenon such as a display of the Northern Lights—which is beyond intellectual understanding and must be understood in the inner life of the soul—it is the manifestation of a soul-spiritual gesture. "Evolution of consciousness" means the evolution of soul-spiritual gesturing, or the evolution of our consciousness in this sense. Intuition means being in touch with the living "being-ness" of things (as Martin Buber might describe the I-Thou relationship). It is the "Grail moment" in everyday life. The Grail moment is a gathering of all the Knights that symbolize human striving in the service of spirit. It means making ourselves available to the spirit working in the moment, experiencing the living being-ness of something with our I, so that we are are fully awake and free in the moment. Then we know what to do. As the poet and essayist Wendell Berry says, "You cannot speak or act in your own best interest without espousing and serving a higher interest" (Sussman, p. 225). Ethical leadership serves that higher interest, and intuition is a tool that helps us to reach that higher interest.

Bernard Lievegoed, the Dutch counselor and businessman, suggests several exercises that can help strengthen a person's ability to work with intuition: 1.) Practice courage and fearlessness in everyday life, so that one can take the intuitive leap when needed. 2.) Presence of mind, often referred to as attentiveness, can help us recognize the moment for intuitive action. 3.) Most intriguing for me at least, Lievegoed suggests that we learn to recognize questions, especially those that are not asked in words, but given by the situation. What is being asked of me here? What was the real question that she seemed to be asking? Why do I find myself in this situation again? (Lievegoed, p. 71).

These exercises have the common quality of speaking of intuition as a momentary opportunity, a time to pay attention to the questions that come toward us, for they contain undiscovered genius. Intuition is not an emotional or instinctive matter. Intuition for the purposes of leadership has more to do with seizing the opportunity when, often after a long wait, the answer or insight arrives. This moment of "arrival" is like Pegasus flying in upon wings from the heavens, yet it is also an internal process. What happens in intuition is that the soul-spiritual is connected to the transparency of the human I. It has a momentary quality and connects with the spark of the divine through the I.

In order to use intuition in leadership, we can ask: As a leader or colleague, should I hold myself back and let the question be lived out by another individual or the community as a whole? This is an ethical question: When do I intervene and when is it best, as my father often says, to let life show what is needed. Can I observe my fellow workers from the vantage point of a Pegasus? If so, the flexing of my intuition may become as growing wings on my feet! For in experiencing intuition, the human being puts aside individual destiny to become an agent of higher powers. Exercising intuition means to live in the moment for the good of others. It is an ethical act.

What was once given to humanity as a "gift from the Gods" is a matter of personal responsibility. In ancient times, human beings were given moral instruction from outside of themselves, first as the imaginative pictures of mythology, as seen in Greece, then later in the teachings of the church. Now we have to find moral spiritual ground within ourselves. We are exposed, as it were, to multiple crosscurrents of greed, desire, and ambition, and the only recourse is to find a counterbalancing response within ourselves. This can be called intuition, conscience, or ethical individualism. Our schools, cultural institutions, and community groups need to see this as a central task: awakening new human capacities in the realm of moral imagination, social responsibility, and the courage to do what is right.

5. Practical Aspects

THE CASE FOR LEADERSHIP MENTORING

A college student is routinely assigned an advisor; a medical intern works under the supervision of a licensed doctor; new teachers in our schools are often assigned a mentor. These practices are well founded in professional life and make eminent sense. Learning does not end with school; in fact, many people look back on their careers and say that they learned more on the job and from life circumstances, peers, and superiors than they ever learned in school.

The notion of mentoring goes well back in history.[1] In the context of leadership ethics, I am intrigued most by the three stages of mentoring found in the craft guilds of the Middle Ages. It is well known that, to become a master in any trade, whether metalwork, weaving, or bookbinding, a person was expected to serve first as an apprentice and then as a journeyman. Working with a proven expert, the young apprentice would do menial tasks, often sweeping the floor and feeding the fire, just for the chance to pick up some of the rudimentary skills needed for the trade. After some time, often several years, the apprentice would gradually be entrusted with the real work of the trade, but always under the supervision of a master. When finally ready, the apprentice could begin to journey about, learning from other masters in distant towns and villages. Only

---

1. I discussed this at length in my book *School Renewal* in a section on mentoring and evaluation.

after this second stage—and by then some were in the middle years of life—would the journeyman be recognized as a new master, able to set up a shop, join the guild of similar craftsmen, and be considered fully established.

This three-step process worked for many years, and was successful precisely because learning was always rooted in practice. Theoretical and practical knowledge was acquired on the job, in context, and through the advice of the master. The apprenticeship process could be applied with positive results in many areas of modern life. One of the reasons school reform has had such meager results is that we have failed to shift the basic paradigm of "school as an academic institution" to action-based learning. Thus, we graduate young people who can take tests (sometimes) but have few of the skills that really matter in the workplace. Schools stuff children's heads with abstract concepts that quickly die on the vine once the test is finished. Learning that is felt, experienced, and lived lasts, whereas learning that is highly theoretical has a short shelf life. This is especially true when it comes to leadership training and development. This is because leaders are, by definition, practitioners. They are people who are on the move, active, and motivated. The worst thing we can do for future leaders is to give them too much classroom training, leadership seminars, and long books to read. I am convinced that the best road to developing leadership is through mentoring.

As mentioned, in the medieval craft guilds, the apprentice often reached middle age before becoming a master. One aspect of the current crisis in leadership is that younger people, who are untried and untested, are making decisions that affect many people's lives. Those on the fast track in Wall Street firms and banking institutions and the whiz kids of the dot-com bubble have contributed to the subsequent problems. Many corporations are letting their older, more mature middle management workers go, just at the age when they can provide good leadership for those under them. They are replaced by younger people, who are paid less and are pushed to work longer hours to contribute to the bottom line. It is too simplistic to generalize and say that all young people are unable to make good decisions or that only older people can. It is a matter of maturity, no matter what the age. Mentoring is one good way to assist in evaluating maturity at any age.

When I visit businesses, schools, and other organizations, I am amazed at how few leaders have received formal mentoring. Most can point to people who have helped them along the way, often receiving invaluable advice. But few of these significant experiences were sanctioned, planned mentoring for leaders. Yet, clearly, with the current crisis in ethics in so many basic areas of our lives mentoring is an urgent need of our time.

There are many ways to develop a leadership mentoring program; in fact, it is an invigorating experience for an organization to do this from the grass roots up, rather than buy into a package deal developed by others. I do not want to be too prescriptive. Here are just a few suggestions to help an organization begin the process:

The criteria for selecting a mentor needs to include the rigor of professionalism as well as the comfort of good personal chemistry. Standards of professionalism can include the amount of experience in leadership roles, interpersonal skills, and a foundation of expertise appropriate to the assignment. To help with personal chemistry issues, for instance, under Templar Associates, I have set up a leadership mentoring service for school leaders that calls for a written assessment, an interview, and an exploratory conversation. Therefore, if the chemistry is not comfortable, either party can back off after the initial conversation. Otherwise, a commitment of ten sessions is needed, so that issues can be pursued and the continuity of conversation can assist in the advice offered. I recommend regular mentoring sessions at least every other week, with an appointed time and email confirmation ahead of time. Email communication can also preview questions to be taken up in the conversation. Some mentors may be open to more frequent email exchanges on substantive issues, but I suggest a live conversation at least once every fortnight as the best way to establish the personal rapport needed in mentorship.

Finally, it is best if schools and organizations support the mentoring process by providing both the time and the funds. This demonstrates support and the fact that there are professional expectations for leadership growth. Too often we ask what leaders can do for us, rather than what we, collectively, can do for our leaders. Organizations need to value leadership development, not only in terms of skill development, but also for ethical decision making. One way to do this is to provide the necessary time and money for mentoring.

After a ten-session series, it is helpful to the greater community if the person who has received the mentoring makes a report to coworkers on the experience, gleaned insights, and any challenges that were identified. This pulls the entire community into the process and adds a "soft" level of accountability to the supporting organization. A report may be brief and must not violate confidentiality. When done well, it can engender greater support for the whole concept of leadership mentoring. In Native American communities, speakers at councils and gatherings always thank everyone for giving them the opportunity to be at the council, and end by saying, "I will take this back to my people." This is a powerful expression of the point of support from a whole community and accountability to the whole community. It means that we never act alone, but are always accountable to others in our group.

One final thought on leadership mentoring: this kind of coaching can enhance ethics in the workplace. Assuming that the mentor is from outside the organization, new perspective and objectivity can be brought to bear on the day-to-day situations faced by the leader receiving the mentoring. Tough questions can be asked and new levels of understanding achieved. For example, there are "streams" that flow between people in an organization. In a school, one might look at the pedagogical stream that flows between two teachers and the financial stream between the treasurer and a board member. These streams come from great distances, and the flow is constant, day and night, nourishing and revitalizing the relationships. From this point of view, it is best to keep the "streams" clear. Yet, when people wear multiple hats (parent, board member, administrator), challenges start to arise. Am I being addressed as another parent or as a board member? If my colleague has a child in my class, is our hallway conversation between two teachers, or is it a parent–teacher dialogue? Crosscurrents like these bring extra challenges, and the only way I know to deal with them is added awareness. Leadership mentoring can help precisely in this realm. People who are very active and those who shoulder many responsibilities are in particular need of outside influence.

There is another aspect to this as well. When we work in one organization, there is a tendency to identify with its culture, the environment, and the practices of others in that organization. Over time, many employees begin to think, feel, and act out of that culture. This can be helpful in realizing the mission of the organization, but harmful in terms of ethics. If too many people identify with a given culture often as it is represented by the top leadership—there is the possibility that they unquestionably follow the accepted practices. They become mini Arthur Andersons or little Sam Waltons, with many of the positive as well as the negative attributes. If, for example, you read the biography of Sam Walton, you will be struck by his optimistic personality, his people skills, and his ability to place himself in the shoes of customers. These qualities were, for the most part, transferred successfully to the organization—even institutionalized, say, in the form of the "greeters" at the entrances. People become more than WalMart employees; they become part of the "family"—somewhat ironic in terms of the corporation's size. But there is also a shadow side to this close identification with the founder; promotions and other matters may not always be as ethical as the company's public image. Under the guise of "family," employees may be expected to subjugate their personal needs for the good of the corporation, which may not, in fact, take care of them in any way whatsoever. Rather than a kind of "group-think," ethics requires individuation, self-reliance, and a willingness to test assumptions, even those of a charismatic leader.

A mentor from another organization can promote ethics by asking probing questions and by getting others to see things outside "the box" of corporate culture. When accompanied by rigorous inner work and personal and professional development, this can promote integrity and honesty. In terms of business application, this might be done by matching the managers in one corporation with those in a similar kind of work at another firm. Even in-house, cross-function mentoring could help open the system to new scrutiny.

ETHICAL DECISION MAKING

What is an ethical decision, as opposed to one that is not? We know that this area of modern life needs much more attention. Because of the recent lapses in business, politics, and religion, many people are looking for new ways of developing ethics in the workplace. There is, of course, an educational component, which has been discussed in prior chapters. In this chapter, I would like to look more carefully at the anatomy of decision making and the role of ethics.

At first glance, there is always the "smell test." As with a long-lost container of food in the fridge, if it smells bad, it probably is bad. The same applies to ethical decisions. Here are a few classic examples:

A CEO and a few close associates propose a recommendation on compensation, bring it up at the board, and then wait for everyone to nod their approval. In these situations, there is often very little discussion, let alone analysis or examination of alternative approaches. The feeling is, "If you support me, you have to go along with this package." Any murmur of opposition, or even a polite question, is treated as a nuisance. There is little freedom in the situation, and, basically, anyone with misgivings has to "stuff it." We recently witnessed extreme examples of this in politics, with various national leaders saying, in effect, "You are either with me or against me."

An employee on a budget committee pushes very hard for a liberal maternity policy, which is eventually adopted. Some weeks later, everyone finds out that she is pregnant. Even if the intentions were basically honorable, there is a feeling of unease about the sequence of events, which leads to a clouded workplace atmosphere.

An employee is struggling, and the outcome of his next evaluation is uncertain at best. Before the assessment, the criteria for evaluating his class of employee are amended, giving him a better chance of survival. Afterward, it turns out that there was a meeting behind closed doors in which the head of another department, who happened to be his wife, intervened on the issue of assessment criteria. No matter what the outcome, the results will now be suspect.

These are the kinds of things that happen in the workplace, and organizations today more than ever are searching for ways to raise the bar of ethical decision making. What is an ethical decision—besides passing the smell test?

WHO IS IN ATTENDANCE

It should be understood without question that those who are part of an employment evaluation and compensation issue should recuse themselves from the actual decision making group. This doesn't mean that they cannot participate in the discussion, since they often have needed information and perspectives. I have always felt that, even when I am very invested in a proposal, if it cannot hold up without me in the room, it is not going to hold up afterward either. There is no problem with calling that person back into the meeting, if some vital information is missing. But at the moment of decision making, the person affected in terms of employment, evaluation, or compensation should not take part, so as to avoid a conflict of interest.

It may seem redundant to say so, but I mean *physically* absent, not just abstaining from the vote. There are ways to influence decisions nonverbally, and knowing who spoke or voted against a proposal can have repercussions later on.

TRANSPARENCY

We live in an open society, yet many of the ethical lapses of recent years occurred because there was less than full disclosure. Budgets, annual reports, and the like should be available to those affected and those who want to spend the time reading them. And they should be presented in a readable, understandable format. The process of decision making is often mysterious and cannot be fully replicated, but the results of the process, the actual decisions, should be transparent. Too much is hidden under the guise of "protection from competitors," and too little faith is placed in the intelligence of ordinary citizens. There are patents and copyrights to protect the rights of our creative colleagues, but business and organizations that serve the public need to be accountable to the public.

For example, any company that serves the public in areas such as water or sewer utilities needs to be accountable and regulated, even when they are privately owned. Corporations that are part of other corporations need to have an open book regarding all the members of all corporations that come under the parent company. These examples and many more show the need for far more transparency in our society if we wish to continue calling ourselves a democracy. Thomas Jefferson said, "The price of liberty is eternal vigilance." As citizens of a democracy, each of us can make a small effort toward ethical leadership by simply requesting information and asking questions of those in positions of leadership.

THE INNER COMPASS

Each of us has an inner compass that moves according to a more or less developed sense for the ethics of a situation. Just as a physical compass directs us toward north, south, east, or west, the inner compass can tell us when we are on course. For some, the instrument is quite crude, only indicating if an act is good or bad and whether there will be consequences. Yet, the compass can move in subtler ways for those who have had the benefit of positive role models and those who have worked toward personal transformation. Not only our actions, but also our words have ethical implications, and a highly developed compass can help us connect our actions with our intentions, our words with our ideals.

Unfortunately, as seen more and more frequently in public life, there are those whose inner compass has been frozen in a glacier of greed. For such people, the flow has stopped, the connections between actions and those affected have been severed, and their actions lead to horrible repercussions. Those who are frozen in their ethics fail to consider, reflect, or dwell on those who might suffer, because the desire for personal gain is so great. Self-service replaces public service.

It is always controversial to speak of current issues. However, one has to wonder: Although the Iraqi people have been told that they will control their oil, why, of all the oil service firms in the world, was Halliburton awarded one of the first and most lucrative contracts to rebuild the oil Iraqi infrastructure? Was it because of its record on environmental issues? Its record on asbestos health–related issues? The value returned to shareholders in terms of stock price? Since this writer can only answer "No" to these questions, it must have had something to do with the fact that the former CEO of Halliburton became the

Vice President of the United States. At the very least, it seems to be a conflict of interest for such a highly placed government official to be so closely connected with the oil firm that will control one of the largest oil sources in the world.

This little book is dedicated to encouraging the personal journey that each of us must take to find ways to develop the inner compass that every person, especially those in positions of responsibility, should be exercising.

WILL POWER

Naturally, there are those who will say that ethics is merely a matter of doing what you know is right, and having the will power to do what you should. Despite the simplistic sound of this admonition, there is some truth in its focus on the will. It is one thing to have good ideas or exercise empathy, but in the end, what matters is how we act. "Actions speak louder than words" is a truism. Many handed-down sayings, proverbs, and axioms contain truth, which is why they have endured. Our actions can be seen as an expression of our will—the force in human nature that provides motive power for activity in life.

Looking more closely at the will, it becomes clear that it lives in different ways in human nature. There is the outer will, manifest in our actions, which connects us sympathetically with the surrounding world. Once we engage, we have more sympathy for our tasks and those joining with us in work. Sympathy as a will force has built many schools, outdoor centers, and village parks. There is a contagious quality to this kind of outer will; people and financial resources are attracted to the effort once there is some momentum.

Yet there is also another kind of will, one that works more subtly—at first, during sleep. This form of will is connected to the organic processes of the human body, such as digestion, that occur even when our waking consciousness is not present. It manifests when it surges up the next day in a feeling soul activity. In Steiner's philosophy, the soul is considered the intermediary between the physical world and the spiritual world. When our unconscious will processes experience during sleep and we awaken with feelings that color our day, we have the opportunity to bring these feelings into consciousness. These feelings sometimes seem outwardly disconnected from the immediate situation, but they influence our actions nevertheless. In contrast to the outer will, this form of will presses up from the sleeping person and pushes things back as a kind of antipathy. In this space, we tend to shut ourselves up within our own being, and we can become self-enclosed in egoism. When this antipathy becomes too strong, it enters our consciousness, or astral body, and affects our relationships to others. Evil people are extreme examples of this; they hate the world and reject it. This is will in negative feeling.

When this "sleeping will" also enters one's mental life, however, it leads to abstraction. It gives rise to "negative judgments, judgments of rejection or denial."[2] I recently observed this in the facial features of someone attending a meeting, and she did not even say a word! In feelings of sympathy, there is life and accomplishment; in the antipathy that rises into conceptual life, there are immobile thoughts. Those with sympathy take part, those with too much antipathy are distant observers. Just look at the last time you made a proposal to a group; they may have all been fine people, but some will have responded out of sympathy and others may have been more distant, at least to begin with. Both can play a role in healthy organizations. From the former we have raw energy; from the later we may hear questions that need to be asked.

In using will power for the sake of right action, it would help if leaders acted as they would like to be treated by others. "Do to them as you would have them do to you." Applying this basic truth could go a long way in this world. Yet for many there is an

---

2. Rudolf Steiner, *The Sun-Mystery*, p. 12.

obvious disconnection between self and others, so that this rule does not seem to apply equally to everyone. It is human nature to have a higher self and a lower self, one aspect that subscribes to ideals, or at least justifications, and one that is more personal, even self-seeking. Even criminals may have elaborate reasons for their crimes; and a respected community leader sometimes struggles with self-interest, the lure of popularity, and the good life. How do we work with this dynamic?

Ancient Greek wisdom spoke of the "mean," or the balance between extremes. For example, we can become totally enthralled by the things of the world or shut ourselves off altogether. On the one side, we do too much in the world in the pursuit of enjoyment and in the acquisition of material comforts; we live life for the moment, to "give yourself a break today." The other extreme is to shut ourselves off with a shell of egoism, filtering everything through our own lens and rejecting anything that does not conform. We get so caught up in ourselves that we begin to lose interest in others. We become hardened, withdrawn, and do too little in the world—perhaps just staying at home with the media that serves Me and only Me.

These are the two sides of will, sympathy and antipathy, taken to the extreme. Both extremes bring a strong possibility for evil or, at least, an over-emphasis that detracts from the social fabric. This is because, in either case, the extremes govern, and the individuality that could bring harmony and balance has become weak. Being gets lost in the world, or *being* becomes lost *to* the world, one-sided, and anti-social. Steiner says that "Goodness consists in avoiding both these extremes."[3] Balance can take a lifetime, even several lifetimes (if one subscribes to the idea of reincarnation), as we swing from one extreme to the other. It is not unusual to see a person in mid-life, for instance, hell bent on earning money or acquiring influence, while in later years that same person might become more spiritual, even giving away

---

3.   Steiner, *The Spiritual Foundation of Morality,* p. 57

much of the hard-earned money. This is a natural balancing within a lifetime. Over several lives, one might enter various situations, so as to eventually accomplish that same balance. This is the "golden mean" of the ancient mysteries, the esoteric teaching passed down, often verbally, from generation to generation. Humans hold the balance between the too-much and the too-little connection to the world. Ethics requires an ability to be both a participant and an observer, active and reflective. Workplace practices that encourage both tend to be healthier.

One final note: I have found that an early indicator of problems can be seen in the social interactions at work and at home. When people share less, criticize or are frequently absent, this is an early sign that the forces of antipathy may be working more strongly. The counterbalancing activity is for someone—anyone—to reach out and build a connection. This can prevent suicide as well as immoral acts of aggression.

PEELING THE ONION

When called for consultation in a school, I often find that the presenting issue is the trigger that set off awareness of a need for change, but that there are other phenomena imbedded in the organization and lurking beneath the surface. Trying to solve the presenting issue without "peeling the onion" further can be unproductive and a waste of everyone's time.

For example, a school called about a perceived absence of professionalism in the organization's communications—teacher to parent, board to community, and administration to teachers. When I visited the school, the initial assessment showed that many of those working at the school spent a great deal of time in meetings, thus negating the assumption that people do not have time to devote to communication. Looking more carefully at the situation by interviewing key players, I found that, beneath the layer of meeting inefficiency, there was a problem with decision making. Groups were unable to reach decisions, which lengthened their meeting time. Peeling the onion further, I found that the failure to make decisions masked a serious lack of clarity about roles and responsibilities, with the result that people could not work together collabora- tively. And under all this, there were significant questions of trust. If people cannot trust one another, it is almost impossible to assign and sanction responsibilities, let alone make decisions with confidence. Once we got started with the trust issues, we found yet another level of concern: people were bringing their personal baggage to the workplace. As things were unpacked from time to time, it created an atmosphere in which many lived in fear of certain personalities. In this particular situation, the onion looked like this:

Lack of professionalism in communications
Long meetings and inefficiency
Problem in decision making
Lack of role clarity and assignment of responsibilities
Little or no collaboration
Trust issues
Lack of personal transformation

How does a leader work with problems caused by a lack of personal transformation among group members? Where is the boundary between personal and professional? When does self- interest conflict with organizational needs or those of the com- munity we serve? If we are to have a healthy workplace in the future, these questions must be addressed by each individual, group, or organization, not by someone else. These questions are a step in the journey toward ethical leadership. The best way I know to address these questions is just that: to ask, inquire, question. Each member of an organization can learn to balance telling and asking, and much can take care of itself in this kind of human interaction.

MORAL TECHNIQUE

Peeling the onion is one way to characterize the process of moving from perception to understanding. Often, people jump from a mere glimpse of the situation to a conclusion, only to be forced to retrace their steps when the outcome shows how flawed that assumption was to begin with. The trick, I have found, is to line up the perceptions, one after another, so that they can begin to speak. One way to do this is to put all of the group's perceptions of a situation on a flip-chart, listed somewhat as in the "peeled onion." The next step is to ask the group to look, observe, and see whether the connections are evident, and whether those perceptions are true for some and not for others. During this stage, I suspend my own judgments as long as possible so that the process can occur naturally.

> Moral action, then, presupposes, in addition to the faculty of having moral ideas, moral intuition and moral imagination, the ability to transform the world of percepts without violating the natural laws by which these are connected. This ability is moral technique.[4]

The world of perception is just as real and important for us as natural laws are for organic processes. When we place the worlds of perception and natural law side by side, we have an opportunity to navigate between them and gain a more holistic picture of reality. Steiner goes on to say that moral technique can be learned just as anything else can be learned. The key element, however, is the activity of the individual in practicing moral action. Here we are speaking of inner activity. For each person, and at each moment of living, there is a new activity associated with moral imagination, working with the perceptions as they were given. Just as we look at a beautiful landscape

---

4. Rudolf Steiner, *The Philosophy of Freedom*, p. 164.

and have to see and see again to take it all in, in the realm of moral imagination, we also have to recreate constantly, from one instant to the next. This is a path of science, not art, or even "ethics" (if we assume the conventional attitude of setting standards). Each individual engages, more or less consciously, in a series of creative acts. We evolve in this respect not as a species, but as self-creating individuals who can become more or less ethical. The evolution of moral life, according to Steiner, can result in ethical individualism, a modern, western path of development. We are not free, insofar as we simply adopt the ethical standards of others; we are free only when we use moral technique to bring our ideal, spiritual intuitions into action. This modern training in ethics is a strenuous, yet real, way to develop skills in this much-needed part of living. For example, a business leader who isn't just listening to the accountant's viewpoint of any given situation, but also takes in the whole picture of the issues and problems, is able to make a moral and ethical judgment.

Other examples might include an architect who works with the topography of the land in designing a house, a farmer who works with the weather, or an artist who lets the medium speak in forming a new creation. Concept and percept become one in creative intuition. As just described, we are continually in the act of creation; we have to be just as alive as a butterfly hovering over an outstretched flower. Ethical leaders need to see clearly, connect the myriad perceptions of everyday life with the discipline of a scientist, tune in through moral imagination, and act skillfully to implement what they know is best. This can put leaders in a lonely spot, but they must stand on secure inner ground. Those who have done so throughout history have moved mountains. Gandhi, for example, always did his inner work first, struggled to understand, and, for example, gave up imported cloth himself, before asking others to do so.

THE INSECURITY OF FREEDOM

This reliance on ethical individualism brings me to a few sentences from the Jewish theologian and philosopher Abraham Heschel. His words resonate more than ever, given today's ethical challenges. These thoughts, given to me years ago on a fragment of paper, can be used as reminders, meditations, or topics for group conversation, because they relate directly to the practice of ethics:

1. The danger begins when freedom is thought to consist in the fact that "I act as I desire" (compulsions). To be what one wants to be is also not freedom, since the wishes of the self-centered ego are determined largely by external factors.

2. Freedom is the liberation from the tyranny of the self-centered ego. Freedom presupposes the capacity for sacrifice (and I might add, self-interest denies free thought).

3. The meaning of freedom presupposes an openness to transcendence, and people have to be responsive before they can be responsible.

4. Human beings are free to be free; we are not free in choosing to be slaves; we are free in doing good; we are not free in doing evil.

5. There is no freedom without awe.

6. We are losing our capacity for freedom. New forces have emerged that regulate our actions. Modern humankind is not motivated anymore, but being propelled. (It might be added, we must love the activity.)

7. Education for reverence, the development of a sense of awe and mystery, is a prerequisite for the preservation of freedom.

8. Freedom is a burden that God thrust upon humanity. Freedom is something we are responsible for.

A final note on practical matters in leadership: Love makes an idea into an ideal. When I am returning home from a business trip, and I think of seeing Ionas again, it is an abstract idea. But when I reach my home and he races into my arms, then my idea of love becomes an ideal of fatherhood. Love is the action that propels us from the abstract thought into an ideal action that moves us to the possibility of change.

6. Inner Dimensions, or Ethics of the Heart & Soul

The following story is told by Andrew Kimbrell in his book *Cold Evil: Technology and Modern Ethics:*

In the early 1970s, at the height of the antiwar movement, I went with a friend to an off-off-Broadway play. The drama, called *The Rescue* ... portrayed the plight of a young American bomber pilot, shot down and injured while flying a mission over North Vietnam. As the drama begins, the pilot, dragging a fractured leg, is fleeing from a band of enemy soldiers who spotted him as he parachuted from his burning plane. He finally collapses and is found by a kindly old farmer, who takes him into his house. The next scenes involve the sagacious farmer and his beautiful young daughter ministering to the pilot's injuries while hiding him from a variety of pursuers, including the army patrol and vengeful neighbors furious about the destruction of their families and farms. Slowly the young man recovers his strength and begins to help around the farm. He learns to respect the life of these peasant people and, yes, falls deeply in love with the farmer's daughter.

The play's denouement is triggered when a band of Green Berets, having illegally entered North Vietnam to rescue the pilot, arrives at the farm. There is a joyful reunion of the Americans, only to be followed by the chilling news that they must kill the farmer and his daughter as security risks. In vain the young pilot pleads for their lives, arguing that they protected him and would never betray him or the rescue mission.

Finally, when it becomes clear that the order to kill is irrevocable, the pilot insists on doing it himself. He takes the old man and his new love into a side room, pulls out his revolver, and after some hesitation shoots himself. (Kimbrell, pp. 4–5)

The pilot's situation presents a classic ethical dilemma. The enemy has become his friend, his rescuers his tormentors. Killing the unknown enemy in war is easier than killing those we have lived and worked with on a farm. In the end, his inner torture is represented by his suicide.

The author goes on to describe the changing face of evil, making the point that it has become less specific to individuals and more generalized in our society:

Here we arrive at a central problem for modern ethics. Evil has never been so omnipresent as it has been over the past century, so perilous to the earth and the very future of humanity. Yet there seem to be very few evil people.... Far from the simple idea of evil we harbored in the past, we now have an evil that apparently does not require evil people to purvey it. (*ibid.*, pp. 8–9)

There is a pervasive quality of modern issues, from global warming to computer viruses: the people behind these things are anonymous, yet millions experience the effects.

Faceless evil leaves people scared, uncertain, and paralyzed. This is the ideal social climate for terrorism, because it plays on trends already at work in society: disconnection, anonymity, and loss of community. The goal of terrorists is not just to kill a few who have been identified as the enemy; rather, it is to intimidate and wreak havoc by creating mass fear. On a psychological level, at least, fear is just as lethal as atomic weapons. For example, people in the United States have witnessed alternating levels of terrorism alerts, from yellow to orange and back again. Each time the warning level changes, we go through a quick recap of the terrible events of 9/11, and airport security is adjusted accordingly. Driving to the Chicago airport during an upgrade to orange, we were stopped at the entrance and searched, even though we were in a typical family car with Mom in the driver's seat. It was strange to have such an ordinary person under suspicion. It left me feeling that things are unpredictable and random, and that nothing we do can really guarantee our safety. This is the kind of fear or terror that is the goal of terrorists.

Within this context, our leaders are left with a more complex situation. Either they take up a new moral, ethical standard, or they revert to the "personification" of evil that worked so well in the past. This harks back to the concept of revenge as played out in *Oresteia* and other Greek myths and plays. Each house takes revenge upon the house that murdered its patrimony. We remain stuck in this mode of dealing with evil and cannot seem to find a way to redeem ourselves. So, without Saddam Hussein, it would have been very hard for President Bush to focus the administration, as he did, on the issue of "weapons of mass destruction." Having at least one person to vilify simplifies a public relations campaign. And it keeps us all from paying attention to internal problems.

It is ironic that, just when President Bush had summoned the necessary financial and military resources to bear down on Iraq, other places around the world, such as North Korea and Jerusalem, flashed out for attention. At times, it seems that evil is everywhere—that we are fighting the world. Even some of our former friends and allies were against the U.S. campaign in Iraq. What lessons can we learn from the events of the past few years? Are we meant to believe that, when in doubt, it is best to go it alone? Somehow the term *coalition* in the context of Iraq did not inspire me as it did during Desert Storm or World War II. I am also concerned that we are sending dubious messages to future generations by embracing the notion of "preemptive war." What would happen if we used the same concept in the streets of New York? Ethically, we are skating on thin ice with this shift in policy.

As stated earlier, after 9/11 we had a great opportunity. Because of the sacrifice of the three thousand who died so suddenly on that day, we gained a vast amount of spiritual capital. People all around the world, even those who seldom look favorably on the United States, sent their condolences. We could have used this spiritual capital to walk the high road of ethical leadership. We could have said to the world, "Let us now unite in our grief and tackle the problems of the Middle East and, out of our unity, impose a peaceful solution on that area of the world. Let us harness our resources to eliminate AIDS in Africa and elsewhere. Let us break out of the cycle of poverty and crime. Let us find a way to support universal health care."

Such issues require huge amounts of human and financial resources, but these could have been summoned if the tragedy of 9/11 had been used for the good of humanity instead of for geopolitical ambition. Instead, how many billions went into bombing the Iraqi people and their land, while destroying many of the remnants of their ancient civilization? It was telling that the world lost major artifacts from the museum of natural history in Baghdad; war destroys the good with the bad. Those in power proved to be politicians rather than moral leaders, and the focus shifted from the war in Afghanistan to Iraq and beyond. Gandhi once said that, if we continue to extract an eye for an eye, the whole world will soon be blind. The tragedy of 9/11 was a double tragedy: in addition to the loss of life, our leaders were blind to the possibility of lasting solutions to world problems.

Weapons of mass destruction, some may argue, are also a world problem. Of course, but to destroy them, why not used other weapons than those proposed by the Pentagon? Violence always leads to more violence, and there may well be a host of new terrorist recruits who respond out of disgust for our military actions. Instead of arm-twisting our "allies" into supporting us, instead of buying support from Turkey and others so that we might use their airfields, we could have simply asked, "How many of you want to do something about weapons of mass destruction?" Through United Nations peace-keeping forces, the nuclear non-proliferation treaty can be enforced, and disarmament can occur in all nations, not just the ones that are not supposed to have the weapons. In a world of nuclear arsenals, no one is safe. Rather than address the core issue, our leaders have simplified things in order to win against an "enemy." If there is anyone who feels more secure as a result of these actions, it is a false sense of security. If we continue to use this same method of physical power against every "problem country" in the world, we will never really succeed. We need to work instead toward a new world order that truly addresses global problems within their context, with the full participation of everyone concerned.

What will it take to regain the high road of ethical leadership? Regrettably, there will be much more suffering before there is a moral uprising that can cause a new Gandhi to emerge. As long as people are only vaguely afraid and living in the lap of luxury, such an awakening is unlikely. It took many years of suffering before the world awoke to the issue of slavery or apartheid or colonial imperialism. Yet those who are aware can begin to make a difference, simply by making their own journey to search for ethical leadership, and by asking questions that will bring a greater awareness into the world.

We cannot just wait it out and hope that things get better, because the consequences are too destructive. As in the battle against apartheid, much was accomplished by a few eloquent writers such as Nelson Mandela, who was willing to endure jail for the sake of his people. His suffering and deprivation created a kind of spiritual capital, and it was put to good use in breaking down the old system in South Africa. The recent President of the Czech Republic, Vaclav Havel, is another example of an ethical leader, one who creates spiritual capital for humanity by sharing his inner abundance, speaking out with courage, and taking up public office for peace and cooperation, rather than just being opposed to things. We need more people with conscience and the intuition to speak out at the right time and in the right place.

We have arrived at my central thesis: Our world cannot successfully address modern challenges without ethical leaders. Such individuals will not be recognized by their popularity nor by their millions in personal wealth, but only by their ability to generate spiritual capital.

We do not have to wait for the next Havel, Mandela, King, or Gandhi. Look at your own community, and you will find people who are doing this kind of work, even if on a smaller scale. They are firefighters, soup kitchen volunteers, and teachers in public and independent schools. Our preoccupation with global issues should not make us junkies of CNN, while we remain insensitive to the good that we can do on a local level. The famous people I have mentioned also lived in villages and worked locally before they were embraced by the world. Rather than being overwhelmed by the problems of the world, we can do something positive in our own communities. We are all interconnected in more ways than we realize. Positive steps in our own communities can ripple out into the greater world. We can do something as simple as refusing to purchase goods made in sweatshops half a world away. This alone can bring pressure upon the corporations who are benefiting from sweatshops and child labor. In fact, each time we purchase a product, we are telling the world economy to "do that again." Each purchase stimulates economic activity, and we can decide what we want to happen on the other side of the world through the ways we use our purchasing power.

We need to step out of our lethargy. Action on behalf of others, no matter how small, is better than none at all. The United States is at a turning point in its history. We either sink into a collection of obese, self-indulgent, arrogant people who simply want to have things their way, or we exert some of the inner drive that founded this nation in the first place. In 1776, this country was ahead of its time in terms of new social forms. Our constitution was truly groundbreaking. Now we need to take a similar leap, not just for our nation, but for well-being of the whole world. We need a "United Declaration of Health," similar to the declaration that started the United States. If nations around the world are able to find common ground on basic needs in terms of health issues or nutrition, it could lead to a coalition for achieving minimum standards in these areas.

Everything that we can do to work for humanity across the lines of nationality will promote real progress. Divisions along national boundaries are a regressive force in the world today, as seen by the divisions between nations prior to the Iraq war. Looking at world problems solely through the lens of nationality is like looking at each toe or finger to find out why someone has the flu. We need a whole-systems approach to world issues. Hunger, health, gender equality, child labor, and environmental preservation cannot be dealt with until we take a holistic approach. Once we are united in our aims, we can find foundations to sponsor and help realize those intentions. As with previous revolutions, once a movement begins, it cannot be stopped.

OBJECTIVE AND SUBJECTIVE

The scene is a beach in south Florida. Louisa, ten years old at the time, is playing with her little brother Ionas, almost two. He spots a shell and runs with delight to pick it up and give it to her. A few moments later, he asks for it back. Such a simple, childlike act! But there is infinitely more to this little incident.

There is extraordinary freedom and grace in his gesture of giving and receiving. The shell was not treated as a possession, but as a miracle to be shared. There was gentleness to his touch and a priceless joy in the sharing. At this early age, he was not self-conscious; his actions were free of personality and completely objective.

Just hold the hand of a young child, and you can sense the objectivity in the child's actions, as if the world and the child form a unity. The transfer of a "thing," such as a shell, is intended to move it, not change it. Further, I have noticed that when Ionas plays with something, his gestures take on the characteristics of the object he is using, For example, his arms move in rounded gestures while playing with a ball; he becomes more ball-like in his movements and posture. His inner and outer being are one. The cosmos is one with the microcosm. The archetypes are still alive in him; never again in life are they so transparent as they are in a child's gestures.

By *archetype*, I mean what forms us from the spirit—the cosmic intention living in us. The gods, or archetypal energies, are "trapped" in matter, and they long to be freed. For most of our adult life, we capture and hold the "light," or spiritual energy, and in doing so, the flow between our inner and outer worlds is interrupted, and these archetypal energies are kept at a distance. Plato said that our lives are lived in the shadows, and that spiritual energy, or the archetype, stands behind reality as a higher reflection. Aristotle saw the spirit's being as ground tone (a musical expression), as being in reality and longing for release through human thought. For example, when we release the gods of love, beauty, truth, and wisdom from matter, we create new spiritual light. When we connect our inner selves with the archetypal energies, it is like a fairytale princess being released from enchantment. They resonate in us and we find an inner calling that allows us to be free to respond. It is an awakening.

> For the World-Thoughts of the Spirit hold sway
> In the Being of Worlds, craving for Light:
> Archai, Archangeloi, Angeloi!
> Let there be prayed from the Depths
> What in the Heights will be granted.[1]

As human beings, we frequently fixate on certain ideas and concepts. This holds the creative spirit of truth and goodness

---

1. Steiner, *The Foundation Stone*, p. 16

captive, and we are given the task of freeing the spirit trapped in matter and craving light. We can do this ourselves by releasing the archetypes through self-awareness. Our task in this life is not to serve ourselves, gain power, or hoard money and possessions; by doing so, we are untruthful to the archetype in us. We twist the light and make the presence of the archetype small. Our real task is to open our gesture, our soul orientation, so that the archetype can resonate in us, and thus we can serve the archetype in ourselves or our groups. Daily living can become a service to the truth.

Eric Fromm, the psychologist, explained this archetypal striving in a compelling way:

> Our capacity to choose changes constantly with our practice of life. The longer we continue to make the wrong decisions, the more our heart hardens; the more often we make the right decisions, the more our heart softens—or better perhaps, comes alive.... Each step in life which increases my self-confidence, my integrity, my courage, my conviction also increases my capacity to choose the desirable alternative, until eventually it becomes more difficult for me to choose the undesirable rather than the desirable action. On the other hand, each act of surrender and cowardice weakens me, opens the path for more acts of surrender and eventually freedom is lost. Between the extreme when I can no longer do a wrong act and the extreme when I have lost my freedom to right action, there are innumerable degrees of freedom of choice. In the practice of life the degree of freedom to choose is different at any given moment. If the degree of freedom to choose the good is great, it needs less effort to choose the good. If it is small, it takes a great effort, help from others, and favorable circumstances.... Most people fail in the art of living not because they are inherently bad or so without will that they cannot lead a better life; they fail because they do not wake up and see when they stand at a fork in the road and have to decide. They are not aware when life asks them a question, and when they still have alternative answers. Then with each step along the

wrong road it becomes increasingly difficult for them to admit that they are on the wrong road, often only because they have to admit that they must go back to the first wrong turn, and must accept the fact that they have wasted time and energy. (Peck, pp. 81–82)

Fromm saw that the genesis of evil is a developmental process, with great emphasis on choice and will. M. Scott Peck (who cites Fromm in his *People of the Lie*) goes on to say that we must also consider the "tremendous forces that tend to shape the being of a young child before it has much opportunity to exercise its will in true freedom of choice" (*ibid.*, p. 82). One of these forces is parental love—whether through its presence or absence—which can affect the self-esteem of the future adult. Without the nurture of parental love, children can become adults who constantly seek love outside themselves, often making decisions based on the probability of being loved by others instead of their own inherent, inner moral compass. To develop self-esteem as an adult, one must develop consciousness.

This leads us to another consideration of love on the path of subjectivity and objectivity. People generally think of love as a highly personal and subjective experience, and this is usually the way it is portrayed in many novels and movies. Yet for the purpose of ethical development, I would like to make the case that there is such a thing as objective love. In addition to romantic love, there is a kind of love that transcends the personal, such as the kind of love that allows a parent to sit on the bathroom floor at 3 A.M., holding the head of a sick child, or the love of a grandparent sharing advice with the unruly teenager in a way that softens even the most obnoxious opinions. There is a love out there that is bigger than birthday gifts, trips to Disney World, or new CDs. Love that has no expectation of personal gain, but is, in fact, willing to risk everything, even reputation, for the sake of what is good. It is a kind of devotional love that provides a model for others and inspires goodness in even the most hardened characters.

We all make many choices every day. But one of the most fundamental is: Do we "buy" our way toward affection, success, and recognition, or do we dare to walk the path of objectivity and love? Each moment of decision presents an opportunity, and how we make the many small decisions affects the spiritual currency available to our leaders and their ethical conduct on our behalf. Every action becomes larger when the members of a county planning board make ethical decisions to preserve their communities against the financial influence of developers or the very real legal threat of their lawyers. That county's leaders must follow with their own ethical decisions, even if only to save face. One person's commitment to ethical decision making can set in motion a whole chain of ethical decisions.

When my son Thomas injured his eye at two and a half years of age, the attending medical team debated whether to remove the eye altogether. After intense examinations, it came down to a judgment call. After discussing all the pros and cons, the lead doctor said, "When in doubt, we have to go with hope," and he operated successfully. That was eighteen years ago to the day as I write this, and Thomas, a sophomore in college, faces another crucial decision. His eye has developed glaucoma, and a series of specialists have recommended an immediate operation, more intrusive than laser, that has a seventy-five percent chance of success. Thomas is against doing it. We have talked about the role of trauma on his decision making—recognizing signs of denial—yet his intuition seems to be telling him not to mess with something he has managed to live with for so many years. As a father, what is my role now? My responsibility and authority are different this time. He has to make the decision, yet I am not exactly a bystander. In my heart, I am as involved as ever.

Do I listen just to the "objective" and respected opinion of specialists? What is the source of Thomas' reluctance? If it is truly intuition, that is also a source of authority. What about my will versus his will? One thing is clear: this is a poignant example of the choices that shape us as human beings. The "sensible" person in me says we need to see another specialist in Boston when my son returns from college in two weeks. Another part of me says, "In the meantime, I need to be as transparent as possible to what speaks through me, both in my night and daytime consciousness." In other words, my ego needs to be removed as much as possible from the dilemma. I do not know the answer, but I can try and be as inwardly awake as possible so the answer can find us. Thus I am working to find a balance between the objective and subjective in making this life decision.

In the meantime, I continue to advocate for changes in child-rearing practices, so that we have the best possible chance of raising children who have the capacities to meet the increasingly complex choices that will face them in the years ahead. By allowing my son to exercise his will in his life choice, I help him develop an inner moral compass. One way to accomplish this when working with children is to let them "do" what they should become, instead of telling them what they need to know to become good human beings. This means their actions and their will shapes their character. How we handle even the little day-to-day matters is important. Are we orienting toward service or selfishness?

For example, in the United States, the educational system is often based on prizes. One school I visited holds a raffle based on ticket sales. The child who sells the most tickets gets a special prize. What kind of message does this send to our children? In another school, a math teacher gives candy to students for correct answers. I know many parents who pay their children for good grades on their report cards. There is no sense of working for the good of the school or working toward an understanding of the math lessons or working for the pride of achievement; rather, all actions are based on the materialistic notion that one must receive a prize for any kind of effort.

Through these actions, we are preparing the way for future Enron executives. They expect prizes, and their expectations become too big for their "classroom." The candy, used so often, is a particularly interesting management technique, since sugar is a quick fix that can, in fact, enhance a tendency toward addictions. How ironic, then, that those same schools often have a health class in seventh grade, after handing out candy for so many years. The sugar diet, beginning with Frosted Flakes for breakfast, begins a trail that leads to quick-fix answers for every area of life. Addictions are formed in the most unusual ways.

Another important aspect of child rearing is children's need for certainty. "This is how it is," not, "What do you want to eat?" Adults often see only the visible part of human nature and fail to consider the spiritual and psychological aspects. I know it is not easy to be a parent in today's world, but, if we want a more ethical future, I cannot stress enough how important it is to achieve a breakthrough on the home front. For example, the concept of "age appropriate" is real. To force two-year olds to tie their own shoes is inappropriate, because they have not yet crossed into self-awareness. Tying a shoe involves the visual ability to focus and see the intersection of two objects. There is a moment in around the age of five when children's drawings show this ability, as they draw more patterns and begin to write letters of the alphabet.

For my birthday recently, my daughter Louisa gave me a beautiful, hand-carved wooden spoon, which is proudly displayed on my office shelf, right next to the hand-carved bowl that my son Ewen gave me for Christmas. The children spent months carving, rasping, sanding, and polishing—all the while knowing that the object would be given to me. They were shaping more than wooden objects. What was going on inside them during this time? Through their intention to lovingly create something for someone else, they were bringing healing forces into the world.

In contrast, picture a person who has all the material possessions that one could possibly want, yet continues to want more. Once the current object of desire is acquired, one just wants more. It could be a Ferrari, a Rolex, or new furniture—the examples do not matter so much as the values they represent. Possessions come to represent a person's self-image, an ersatz, replacement self. Instead of finding Self, these people acquire things that hold a vague image of what advertisers claim to be Self. Rather than one's identity arising from within, these things form an external identity. But when there is a recession or job loss, the whole edifice crumbles, leading to depression, drinking, or worse.

But the greatest concern is the way so much material longing affects the soul. Desires increase, and a person can become obsessed with a craving that takes over. It is no longer the car itself that matters, but the stimulation of constantly acquiring new things. The nightmare for such people is to become cut off from the gravy train—and thus the golden parachutes, signing packages, yearly bonuses, and stock options. These are all symptoms of a powerful addiction.

There is an intimate connection between the soul and the sensations of the physical body. It is normal for the senses to inform the soul, whether it is a beautiful sunset or a delicious spinach salad. The soul is richer for the manifold impressions that flow toward it from the physical senses of touch, taste, sound, and so on. But when it becomes one-sided, problems arise. A person with too much simpatico (a term used by the artist Collot d'Herbois) has too much sympathy for satisfying desires. Satisfaction becomes an end in itself, rather than a means to enrich the soul life. This simpatico is a kind of subjective will that needs constant feeding. Like a fire in the furnace, the hotter it gets the more wood it consumes.

The kind of person who has this excess simpatico is often quite good with people, wonderfully outgoing and sociable. As I have learned from my wife Karine, if we relate this attitude to the world of natural color as symbolic of aspects of the soul, it would express the shiny reds and golds that we relate to warmth and even joy. Yet within the color and soul spectrums, the blues would be missing. This is the place in the soul that has to do with letting the outer world be. It allows us to reflect and digest experiences and let go of attachments and excessive involvement. We tend to have soul habits that go either in one direction or the other. We need to widen our spectrum to include both the reds and the blues. By nurturing the soul this way in times of quiet, we can also learn to stand in the quiet place of green. From this vantage, we can reenter life with a more complete soul involvement. Thus the simpatico of red needs the cooling of blue. Warmth and compassion of soul must always go hand in hand with clarity and focus of thinking. There is wisdom in the blues!

In *The Christian Mystery*, Rudolf Steiner said, "How does it help someone who has fallen and broken a leg when fourteen people stand around overflowing with compassion and love, but not one of them can set the leg? None of them is of any use. But the one who can do this can help" (p. 84). We need compassion and wisdom that can become action. Ethical actions can arise on their own and do not need to be taught if our view of life arises from spiritual practice. We need the purification and balanced soul that allows all the colors, the fullness of humanity that is called for in a given situation. Human beings need to think less in matter and more in spirit.

THE SOUL AND SPIRIT OF ETHICS

As the keeper of the past, the soul is continually collecting treasures for the spirit. My ability to distinguish right from wrong is due to the fact that as a human being, I am a thinking being capable of grasping truth in my spirit. The truth is eternal; even if I were continually losing sight of the past and each impression were new to me, the truth could still always reveal itself to me again in things. But the spirit in me is not restricted to the impressions of the moment; my soul widens the spirit's field of vision to include the past. And the more my soul can add to the spirit from the past, the richer the spirit becomes.

The soul passes on to the spirit what it has received from the body. Thus, at every moment of its life, the human spirit carries two very different elements—first, the eternal laws of the true and the good; second, the recollection of past experiences. Whatever it does is accomplished under the influence of these two factors. Therefore, if we want to understand a human spirit, we must know two different things about it—first, how much of the eternal has been revealed to it, and second, how many treasures from the past it holds.

In this quote from Steiner's early book *Theosophy* (pp. 68–69), I was struck by the statement concerning the ability to distinguish between right and wrong, described as a capacity for "grasping truth in my spirit." Let us examine this more closely.

In most schools and, indeed, in most workplaces today, the emphasis is on developing skills, or "skill sets," that will help individuals compete successfully, as measured in standardized tests and in later earning power. Skills are important, of course, but they are by nature defined and focused on immediate outcomes, and they come to us from the outer world. Skills come at various levels. Typing is a skill and, for me, it is at a moderate level. Skills can be changed with time. For example, reading is a skill that I did not develop until around the age of ten. We may assess our skills differently, but they can always be measured. Driving is a skill I perform quite well (if you don't ask my wife). In contrast, a capacity is a more generalized ability, less focused on immediate needs and yet capable of growing with time. Capacities include imagination, problem solving, social sensitivity, and, yes, thinking.

The wonderful thing about capacities is that they tend to increase and mature with time. A person who as a child created many imaginative drawings of houses, bridges, and landscapes may become an architect. Rather than train to be an architect at age six, the best preparation is to have experiences in school that foster imaginative work with color and form, observation, and representation. It sounds absurd that anyone would want to enroll a six-year-old in an architecture school, yet that is what happens in schools that focus on skills and ignore capacities.

In regard to the capacity to think, we often overwhelm children with memorization and regurgitation at the expense of cognitive development. In a history or social studies class, children might be asked to remember numerous facts about the life of Thomas Jefferson, then demonstrate this knowledge on a test. The grade will reflect the student's skill level in memorization of what the teacher presented and what was retained from readings. In contrast, a class that works on the development of capacities might not give any tests, but include many vivid details in the life of Thomas Jefferson, as the students engage in active research, storytelling, projects, and conversations. After several days of involvement, students might be asked, "Why were there so many 'chapters' in Thomas Jefferson's life?" Their answers could come verbally, in writing, or both, but the emphasis would be on processing the information, and on their open-ended, creative responses. This approach tends to encourage their capacity to think.

The latter approach to learning is more than pedagogy; it is a link to distinguishing between right and wrong. With healthy thinking, people acquire the capacity to grasp the truth of a situation. This cannot be inculcated through a list of "do this and don't do that." It needs to be reacquired each time. What works in one situation may not be effective in another, as history so graphically informs us. Evil is often something that is merely out of place in time. Certain social practices, such as slavery, that were considered appropriate in the past, have proven to be anything but good. Modern dictators often borrow social practices that are no longer considered appropriate and try to perpetuate them. The moral sense for the truth of a situation requires a fresh, contemporary analysis of each moment. An ethical leader sees the world with a fresh perspective and penetrates the phenomena with open-minded, fresh cognition. A tyrant uses a situation to manipulate and distort reality for personal gain.

"As the keeper of the past, the soul is continually collecting treasures for the spirit." This earlier citation from Theosophy contains much in terms of the soul and spirit of ethics—a notion of how the soul nourishes the spirit. This is a fascinating concept. I have always marveled at the truly great spirits of humanity: Mahatma Gandhi, Martin Luther King, and others. Were they simply great to begin with, or did they do something along the way to call forth greatness?

In studying their biographies, I am struck by the ways in which they seized and made something of situations that had also been presented to countless others. Other Indians suffered from English imperialism, other blacks from segregation. Yet these two men worked with these situations in a new ways. They used their capacities. And they assimilated their soul experiences most profoundly. What they saw moved them. Rather than become sentimental, they did their own inner work based on what they saw as injustice around them. They grew from the experiences of their lives. And these soul dimensions then fed the spirit until it became so abundant that it spilled out over all of humanity.

There is another interesting connection between these two men. Martin Luther King was influenced by Gandhi, who had been influenced by the American transcendentalists Ralph Waldo Emerson and William Henry Thoreau. Emerson and Thoreau were indirectly influenced by the German writer Schelling, who had access to translations of ancient Eastern philosophical and spiritual texts, some of which came from India. For me, this says that ethics and ethical behavior have a spirit life of their own and continue to manifest for humanity, no matter how hard we try to destroy it.

We live in a time when we need a Gandhi or a King to take the lead in solving the problems of the Middle East and elsewhere. But what can we do? We can begin by being conscious and alert to a new kind of leader, one who very well may not be a politician or public person at the moment. We can begin to define the characteristics of this kind of leader, and through our active support of the democracy we live in, we can begin to require these characteristics of our leaders. Most important, we can work to enhance the riches of soul transformation that feed the human spirit of each one of us.

What enhances the riches of the soul? My wife Karine has made a study of color as symbolic of soul aspects, and we often discuss ideas like this as we pursue our personal and professional journeys. My question to her on one occasion was, "So how can human beings today enhance the riches of the soul?" She began by saying that this involves embracing the entire soul and deepening its life in a variety of ways. This reminded me of a storybook with wonderful, simple pictures that I had been sharing with our little Ionas recently: the story of the Seven Ravens. Early on, there is a painting of the seven brothers grouped around a well looking for the pitcher they dropped into the water. Having lost the pitcher, they fail to return home with water to baptize their little sister, which prompts their father to curse them and wish that they would turn into seven ravens—which, of course, happens. The beginning of their soul journey is the pitcher falling into the water. It is only the intervention of a journey by their little sister that eventually transforms them back into human beings.

Why did the image of the pitcher in the well speak to me? It is a defining moment of choice; it shows that the task of each of us, as human beings on earth, is to take hold of life and make something of ourselves. Once we have dropped the pitcher, what is the next step? We are not here just to live a materialistic life. Spiritual work can mean directing our attention and inner resolve toward certain tasks, including the transformation of what we are given in life. This happens on several levels; penetrating our lower nature with the I, or ego, is one level. As described in School Renewal and elsewhere in anthroposophic literature, we have a physical nature, a body of life forces, and a consciousness body. To the extent that we bring our intentions and resolve to bear on the lower aspects of our nature, the higher member, the I, can bring about transformation.

Just as the seven brothers watched as the pitcher plunged into the well, the human I, the vessel of our consciousness, observes and experiences as it plunges into and penetrates the lower members of our consciousness. Falling is relatively easy; it is the return trip that takes effort. In the story, it is the sister who takes a long journey to find and release her brothers through faithfulness. Along the way, the father's anger is transformed, and the brothers become human again. Through the sister and the symbolic feminine nature of the pitcher, we learn that it is the feminine, intuitive side of ourselves that allows the higher self to return from the depths. As noted in chapter five, this speaks to the importance of the intuitive will and its relationship to ethical leadership.

One excellent means of bringing about this transformation of consciousness is through the practice of the arts. When modeling with clay, one exercises transformative power over a physical substance. In painting with watercolors, the colors flow across the wet page, and the life forces (energy levels) are worked with by the intention of the person using the brush. As for music, whether singing or playing an instrument, one is working with the consciousness of feelings, the astral element of human nature. Just take some time to listen to various musical styles, whether jazz, folk, or classical, and you can experience the astral consciousness, or feelings, of the composer and musician. And, by listening, our own consciousness is affected. Because the astral consciousness, according to Steiner, is part of the soul, it is an inward experience, and the "genius" of the music penetrates to the deepest recesses of our being. One feels, breathes, and even thinks differently when listening to Mozart or Brahms. Likewise, when Pavarotti sings, he is there with me in the car, no matter how many miles separate us. After listening to music, especially live concerts, I feel refreshed and renewed. There is an inner mobility of energy coming from the art form that allows me to experience, and then put into practice, the transformational work needed to be the person I want to be— that is, if I make a conscious effort to do so. The soul can become richer by deepening and transforming the experiences we are given, especially through the arts.

When we experience a moment like a pitcher falling into the well, how do we work with such events in life? For some, they are seen simply as luck, good or bad; for others, they become material for growth. In my study of history, outstanding people have become known to us not so much through their native, given talents, but through what they did with that talent in their lives. Queen Elizabeth I of England is a good example. She was just one more princess, born among numerous royal offspring. She was thrown into the Tower of London, and eventually ascended the throne when England was at a financial, military, and cultural low point. Yet, through the force of her personality and her ability to learn on the job, by the end of her reign she had turned everything around. Her biography is an excellent example of the transformation of life experiences and the greatness of spirit that can emerge.

If we encourage not only skills but also capacities, and if we practice transformative action in our lives, we will also recognize it in others. Once we gain the capacity to live in eternal truth through the transformative power of thinking, we will have an excellent chance of growing ethical leaders. Leaders such as Mahatma Gandhi and Martin Luther King, who have grown in the human encounter of soul richness and spirit greatness are the kind of leaders our world needs today.

DISCONNECTION AND DISTANCING

In considering the inner dimensions of an ethical leader, there is another factor: disconnection. In overly abstract college education, in military strategies that refer to civilian casualties as "collateral damage," and in public policies that destroy the environment, there is one common denominator—a quality of disconnection and distance. Policies are not considered holistically, but disconnected pieces of reality are used to justify any means. For corporations, the goal is to increase profits; for Congress, reelection; for most schools, higher test scores. A vast gap emerges, a Grand Canyon that separates cold calculations and those in power from the public and the environment affected by their machinations. This is the chasm into which all ethical considerations fall from sight. It's like a person who is smart and has the will to succeed, but has no heart to consider the human implications. Those who are all head and will are often successful in the world, impulsive, and headstrong, with a type-A, take-charge character—but may be unreal and lacking warmth. This type of person is always out there in the world, but not particularly reflective or inward. Solutions are found for manipulating reality. In contrast, the doorways of the heart, when opened, include conscience, intuition, and many of the qualities described throughout this text.

To a large extent, we are still working with the old dogmas and outer rules instead of inner realities. We can talk about war in the Middle East without comprehending its real meaning. We can say "yes" to war because of our abstractions. If a bomb actually fell in our hometown, war would be a different reality. If we could see the suffering of a child left without parents because of strife, we would see all human frailty. We tolerate terrible things because they are abstract and far away. We watch the world's horrors on television, and it all begins to seem the same, with no reality of actual presence. It is a cool, if not cold, medium.

We need to humanize our human spirit and fill it with love and striving. To do so, we need a larger picture, one that includes a new perception and sensory awareness that brings the outer world inside. Then our heart-permeated light will shine out again, creating new outer substance for humanity. Light in and of itself can be harsh. When we allow the light to pass through the humanizing aspect of the heart, it regains the warm reds and oranges of the spectrum. We combine the clarity of light with the warmth of the heart. To begin this process, we can ask: In what ways am I disconnected from my family, my community, or my environment? How can I begin to humanize my interactions with others in my daily life?

I am not alone in looking at these phenomena. Andrew Kimbrell has the this to say about workplace ethics and distancing:

Ethical distancing and ethical problems of scale are not limited to high-impact, military technology. The behavior and nature of modern technocracies, business, and government organizations are equally illustrative of this cold evil. Witness how corporations, now working on the global scale, routinely make calculated decisions about the risks of the products they manufacture. Typically, they weigh the cost of adding important safety features to their products against the potential liability to victims and the environment and then make the best "bottom line" decision for the company. More often than not, safety or environmental measures lose out in this calculation. As for people or nature, they have been "distanced" into the numerical units relegated to profit-or-loss columns. The corporations then decide how many units they can afford to have harmed or killed by their products.

We witness daily the way the modern corporation has become distanced in time and space from its actions. A pesticide company has moved to another country or even gone out of business by the time—years after it has abandoned its chemical plant—the local aquifer and river have become hopelessly polluted, fish and wildlife decimated, and there is a fatal cancer cluster among the families relying on the local water supply. The executives of a tire company are thousands of miles or even a continent away and do not hear the screech of wheels and the screams as their defective tires burst and result in fatal crashes....

Cold evil's distancing is also profoundly present in those who work for corporations and other technocracies. Our minute and specialized jobs have separated us from ethical consideration of our collective work. Whether processing financial statements at a bank, riveting at a Boeing plant, litigating for a large law firm, or delivering on-line data to corporations, most people's work represents a tiny cog in the great machine of production. As a result, we become psychologically numbed and removed from the ultimate consequences of the collective work being done. We fall into what E. F. Schumacher termed "the sullen irresponsibility" of modern work. (Kimbrell, p. 17–19)

This whole discussion raises the possibility that decreased connections and loss of meaning in work has resulted in a work force that is ethically stupefied. Many people no longer see the bigger picture, because their jobs are so pitifully fragmented. A person driving the delivery truck may not even have the information, let alone the inclination, to put together the pieces and see that the truck helps deliver parts that keep a nuclear plant going. Labor has been so broken up that it is almost impossible to trace the various strands of a product back to their origin. We end up buying products we do not know or understand. We use them without seeing the connections. This situation makes it harder than ever to act ethically.

A hundred years ago you could walk downtown and meet the person who sold and cut the wood used to make the table you intended to buy. It mattered who stood behind the craft; a person's reputation was a vital currency. If there was a problem, the craftsperson would most likely fix the product while you waited. The individual and the product were connected. Payment for such service might have been refused, but knowing the time spent on your behalf and that there was a family to support, you might have insisted on paying.

How different it is today. There are "800" numbers and so-called help lines to call for service—often busy—and it seems that most products are pieced together from all over the world. The result is that true responsibility is often evaded, and those involved in creating the product are obscured. A stupefied workforce and a fragmented labor picture provide an ideal basis for ethically-challenged leaders. Why? There is less chance that they will be held accountable

In contrast, we have examples of business people who stand for humanity, as did the owner of a factory that burned down in Malden, Massachusetts some time ago. Rather than dismiss all the workers, he kept them on the payroll at his own expense, knowing that they and their families had to continue living. When the factory reopened a year later, he did not have to worry about finding qualified help or negotiate with unions. They were united, not against management, but with management.

"IT'S LONELY AT THE TOP!"

When the owner of the factory in Malden decided to follow an ethical path, he did so on his own authority. Leaders often walk a lonely path. Frequently, they are on their own, with little chance to share their struggles and aspirations. We can try to escape from the loneliness, but it usually catches up with us, especially at moments of big decisions, and usually when everyone we are responsible for appears to need something. It can seems as though people think a of a leader as the inevitable "pocket lady" at a holiday fair. The hands keep reaching out for something that the leader is simply expected to produce.

Instead of running from the loneliness of leadership, we can make loneliness an object of observation. So much today keeps us whirling in activity that we rarely hear the "gentle possibilities we carry within the inner circumference of our soul-space, whose landscape is pervaded by our very own color of loneliness" (Pietzner, p. 17).

In *Lonely Generation and the Search for Truth*, Carlo Pietzner describes how the experience of loneliness "means also to become aware that it is a kind of mantle, the mantle of our ego" (*ibid.*). Within this mantle there is a hollow space, through which the whole world passes as a reflection. One can feel that the many emotions, sensations, and impressions moving in that hollow space are not really "me." We sense that there is something more to the story we are living each day. A single biography on earth may not encompass the larger goal, the full story. So loneliness invites us to see that

> within the hollow space of one life, of one attempt to become a person, the totality cannot be contained. It begins to dawn, that the loneliness of one person, however complex, special, individual, is yet nothing but a hollow space and not the "I," and that the true totality of the complete individual must be infinitely greater and, therefore, must be seen—even though our eyes cannot yet see it—as reaching from one earthly life to another, from one incarnation to the next. (*ibid.*)

Thus, embracing loneliness offers an opportunity for inner reflection, and this can help us make ethical decisions. Another aspect of this fear of loneliness is that leaders are often surrounded by subordinates who never allow accurate information to reach the top. Leaders may have no idea what is really going on, and, consequently, decisions are made for which those in charge feel no responsibility. Being lonely means having to take responsibility for one's actions. Once a person takes responsibility, paradoxically and mysteriously, there is no longer a sense of loneliness, but of relief and a response from those affected.

KARMIC CONSIDERATIONS

Finally, whether we live more than one life or simply carry our own past with us, leaders should look at interpersonal dynamics from a broader perspective. This helps leaders see, in a new way, the currents flowing through the workplace. For example, administrators and CEOs must frequently mediate conflicts. Whether simple misunderstandings or major differences on fundamental issues, conflict can tear an organization apart. In many cases, organizations have failed to recognize their potential, largely because they are held back by unresolved conflict between members of the organization. It is often not overt, and in my experience, it usually tends to be more subtle. Nevertheless, it frustrates or blocks the larger vision. Conflict is a fact of life in an organization, and occasional, direct mediation does not always reach real resolution. This is where I find the karmic perspective helpful.

Rudolf Steiner, in his spiritual investigations, observed that those we meet at mid-life are often the very people who were once our parents and family members in the past life.[2] Consider the implications of this statement. We all know something about family dynamics: intense, instinctual love; sibling rivalry; the pull of heredity versus individuality. Consider your own birth family and recall the relationships and feelings associated with them. Also remember—perhaps at the beginning of dating as a teenager—wishing that your boyfriend or girlfriend were different, more like the person of your fantasies. This yearning to transform our childhood relationships creates tremendous forces of will in the soul. And yet, for the most part, we cannot change the circumstances of our birth family, and so that yearning remains largely unfulfilled. This then spills into our next life, in which we may look for a workplace where we might find a chance for relational transformation.

From one life to the other, "conditions are dislodged and experiences that were caused in the past can be resolved" (*ibid.,* p. 62). Whether we believe this or not, it is wise to note the people and events that seem familiar to us. We may learn more about ourselves and see our experiences in a new way. It is an interesting thought that we have sought out colleagues who often were connected to us as family members a lifetime earlier. It takes the loosening of death and rebirth to give us the wherewithal to take this work further. Issues can be worked on once

---

2. Rudolf Steiner, *Anthroposophy in Everyday Life,* p. 60.

they come up in the form of conflict, which is, unfortunately, too often the case. Or we can take these karmic realities seriously and begin to provide opportunities for adult work that allows a more constructive approach. By asking for self-administration in Waldorf schools, Steiner was really saying that it matters how you relate; make it part of your mission. If you self-administer, or if you want your organization to be more than just an institution, you have to interrelate in a more active way.

The inner dimensions of ethics begins with the choices we make each day and our awareness of those choices. When practiced with full conviction, ethics is highly practical. Inner work leads to transformation, which leads to a new conviction—the possibility of working from the heart as ethical individuals. We have heard the saying, "We cannot change the world, only ourselves." The paradox, however, is that, when we change ourselves, it ripples out in ever-widening circles into the world at large.

7. Sun and Moon

In the journey of our search for ethical leadership, we have discovered many of the signs and symptoms that indicate the need for a return to ethical leadership. Along the way, we have looked at ways to promote ethical leadership in our schools and with our children. As our journey progressed, we discussed the practical aspects of ethical leadership, and then moved on to some of the inner dimensions. Now we will delve more deeply into a spiritual approach to this question.

The first Waldorf school, founded and directed by Rudolf Steiner, was established for the chilren of the workers at the Waldorf cigarette factory. Owing to the support of Emil Molt and the association he helped found, there was no tuition as we know it in North America. Even today, when I visit Waldorf schools in Europe, there seems to be less of a barrier between the general population and the families of the schools.

For example, a few years ago I gave a talk at a conference in Flensberg, Germany. The school festival (May Day, as I recall) was celebrated in the open market downtown. I stood on cobblestones, surrounded by shops, churches, and old houses, while the Waldorf school classes performed on an improvised stage at one end of the square. Townspeople and shoppers came and went, some sat to watch, and others picked up literature on a table. Parents circulated freely. The children did some wonderful performances of songs, movement, and dramatic pieces, as they do in the school assemblies here in North America. As I stood there, I sensed that this was truly a village school.

In June 2002, my family's visit to England happened to coincide with the Queen's Golden Jubilee. We were caught up in a parade that started downtown and wound its way through the streets and up the hill. There were children on bicycles and others on homemade floats, as the townspeople followed. The whole procession ended up on the grounds of the Michael Hall School, where booths were set up, with amusements for children of all ages. It was possible to sit on the veranda of the old manse and have a cup of English tea. The crowd was ninety percent townsfolk, with only a scattering of the Waldorf school community. This, again, was a community event.

In Johannesburg I attended the market on the grounds of the Michael Mount Waldorf School. They have a section of land, permanently set up so that farmers, artists, and artisans can sell goods each week. One evening each month, they have a special musical event with open-air cafes and booths open to the evening. I was delighted to hear that the school, beset by reverse immigration and a large population of needy children, derives a substantial portion of its annual budget from the fees and commissions earned through the fair booths. It was a free enterprise supporting independent education.

Since colonial days, the United States has a tradition of private education, beginning with William and Mary College, Harvard University, and others. This has, in some cases, allowed excellence and freedom from governmental control. Yet this has come at a price—literally—through the high tuition at private colleges and secondary and elementary schools. High tuition restricts attendance and leads to the separation of economic classes, which is addressed only partially by scholarship programs. Even when financial aid is plentiful, some groups in our society do not apply in large number because of a perception of elitism. Consequently, our public-private split in education creates barriers between people. Just consider the Ivy League old-boy network in contrast to the "townies" in many college communities. This divide should be addressed more effectively, without watering down our educational institutions to the common denominator of mediocrity. Can we have excellence *and* equal opportunity? We can; I have cited examples of schools in various parts of the world that have achieved excellence while practicing a policy of social inclusiveness.

What are the necessary conditions for a school without walls? What is the ideal parent-teacher relationship? In the three examples I mentioned, the teachers were involved only in regard to the children; parents and community members managed the events. How do we create the conditions for real community schools?

As we look for health in community life, we might look first at the health of those who make up the community. By liberating individual human potential, we can create new possibilities for individual interactions and community experience. A useful exercise is to observe the following: We all have the soul capacities of thinking, feeling, and willing. Are you mostly a feeling or a thinking type of person, or a person of will? When there is a task that needs to be done, do you think about it first, or do you express a feeling about it? Or, do you jump right in and do it and reflect later? There are no wrong and right answers, but it is helpful as an exercise in self-observation.

If I work mostly out of my thinking capacity, the strength I bring to group work might include clarity, focus, and insight, yet the shadow side could be a penchant for unnecessary comments, over-analysis, and even criticism. If I am primarily a feeling person, I might easily establish empathy and harmonize social situations. Yet the shadow side could be emotionality, a tendency to go too far with expression and reactions, even to minor incidents. If I am mostly a person of will, and if that will is harnessed, I can virtually move mountains, accomplish things under the most adverse conditions, and generally impress myself on the world. The down side occurs in conflict, when I might fight only for my own agenda, staking out a narrow band of work that satisfies my desires and ignores the needs of the group. Willful people often want to do their thing and avoid too much interference. We can always choose which of these capacities we are willing to work with, but on an instinctual level, especially when we are tired or too busy, we tend to operate in a certain, preferred mode.

The next step of the exercise is to look at a particular group task or situation and ask, "What soul capacity does this task, person, or situation require of me? I hear a colleague speaking with a lot of feeling, and it calls on me to respond with reflection, to bring balance to the situation." Or, "Here is an analytical response that needs to be brought to life with warmth of feeling." In this way, we can become aware of the soul capacity another person is exercising, and we can meet it with an equal but balancing soul capacity. A good leader is aware of the capacities of individuals involved in group work. In a school community meeting, responding to the soul capacity a parent or teacher generally means starting where that person is at the moment—whether the individual is self-aware or not—and working from there toward the wholeness of relationship that arise from balancing our soul capacities.

This leads to the third step: to the greatest extent possible, we try to do the balancing ourselves as part of our individual expression, rather than depending on others to do this. A good leader works to develop thinking, feeling, or willing as needed, working toward greater self-mastery. This inner work has the effect of enlivening the spiritual environment and making the community of human relationships more interesting to the spiritual beings who want us to succeed. Ethical leadership is the ability to take two steps in self-education, while taking one in support of others. For example, before I can write, I need to clean my room, order my materials, and collect myself inwardly. In the words of a Danish proverb: Order your "backcountry" before sailing out into the world. Parenting, teaching, and serving as a therapist comes from one's "surplus"—inner resources accumulated over time. We have to make our lives work well enough so that we have something extra to give, and this requires inner work. There is nothing more practical and helpful to community life than freely and willingly ordering our own lives and establishing self-equilibrium before looking to others.

In our journey for ethical leadership, in order to create community we need to move beyond individual paradigms and examine the deeper issues. Thanks to Anthroposophy, we can take in the larger cosmic picture by examining two types of energy, as symbolized by the Sun and the Moon. One way to do this is to look at the cultural epochs described by Steiner and focus on the changing relationships to the Sun. This spiritual wisdom can be applied to the leadership dynamics in community and the development of a new ethics.

In ancient Persia, the Sun was seen as the divine source of Light, or Spirit. Zoroastrianism is characterized by the duality of good and evil, light and dark. There was a struggle between the forces of light and darkness, personified by the spiritual beings of Ahura Mazda and Ahriman.[1] Ahriman tried to rule humanity through deception, greed, and dissension. People were directed to look for material gain through the mechanization of work and one-sided development of the senses. In contrast, Ahura Mazda tried to lead humanity toward unity with the spiritual worlds, promoting a healthy relationship to all living things and a wholesome use of the senses. God could be found in the Light, or, to put it another way, God could be experienced as an expression of radiant light.[2]

To access this radiating light as an expression of the divine, the following may be used as a leadership meditation. A good leader has a spiritual life. Find a special spot in nature, one not frequented by others and away from the bustle of everyday life. In doing so, we follow a practice of native peoples everywhere,

---

1. See *School as a Journey,* chapter 5
2. Rudolf Steiner, *The Sun Mystery in Relation to Human Evolution,* pp. 13–17.

who prefer sacred places in nature for prayer and meditation. Once in a comfortable position, use the awareness you usually direct toward all your consuming daily concerns, and focus it instead on inner peacefulness. When the soul has been quieted, look out at the play of light as it meets the rocks, trees, and plants. Observe the light-filled spaces and those that are in the shade. Let the contrast develop so strongly that there are two distinct experiences: light and shadow. At this point, I always feel gratitude that both light and shadow exist in the world; colors would not be so rich if light and darkness did not encounter each other. Then, as the last step, fill your consciousness with these words: "God is Light; Light is God." Let this truth reverberate throughout your whole being. Then return to inner quiet and walk home, aware of any difference in the way you feel.

Ancient Egypt was another culture for which the Sun was of primary importance. It had a strong natural presence out in the desert, in the land of pyramids and ruling pharaohs. With the flooding and receding waters of the Nile, sun and water combined to allow plant life along a narrow stretch of land, providing the food to support human life. For ancient Egyptians, the Sun was seen as the divine source of Life. Egypt's burial customs and its focus on the details of the life after death was an indication that they understood the difference between life in this world and life in the world one reaches after death. The great pyramids and tombs are monumental testaments to the significance of crossing the threshold between life and death. The soul's entry into the spirit world at death is vividly shown in the many beautiful paintings in those ancient tombs.

We can also deepen our understanding of the dynamics of life and death by using the following leadership meditation as a way to connect with the teaching of an ancient culture. As indicated in *How to Know Higher Worlds*, Steiner suggested contemplating an object that is alive and growing, and then one that has died. By observing a leaf on a tree or a stick on the ground, for example, the exercise can be factual at first—just seeing what is there as a stick or green leaf. After a while, that which is alive begins to stir the soul with a feeling of expansion and a sense of the sun shining out into the world. The dead stick, in contrast, seems to contract, merely reflecting light off the surfaces, just as the Moon reflects sunlight. As with the other meditations, it is best to let these two experiences resonate in feelings and avoid too many conclusions.

So, why call these exercises "leadership meditations"? Of course, they can be done in many situations, but I will indicate a leadership context for this last exercise. If a person working toward ethical leadership were to do this exercise for many months, the opportunity might arise to use the acquired soul forces in a practical way. For instance, I have come to realize that, when working with groups, there are "formative" activities and "diminishing" activities; both occur as a natural part of life. A formative activity might be strategic planning, vision work, program development, singing together, or a retreat. In contrast, activities that diminish and use up human resources are business meetings, scheduling, and personnel matters. Both types of activity are part of any organization. It really gets exciting in terms of ethics when the leader is able to sense a need balance and know when to intervene on behalf of healthy group dynamics and development.

Ethical leadership is not just a matter of avoiding misdeeds (as is often portrayed in literature on the subject), but also providing bold intervention on behalf of group health before things get out of hand. When a group goes too far down the path of "diminishing returns," people become fatigued and begin to work from their shadow side, and then power plays and manipulation set in. Every group and situation can be seen from the life-death dynamic, either building or diminishing, and too much of one or the other leads to imbalances. Too much of the life pole can result in a kind of hedonistic chaos, in which everyone is doing his or her own thing—but on a collision path. Ethical leadership intervenes before it's too late. To do this, one needs the kind of awareness that can come from the meditations I've mentioned.

In Greece, one can rejoice in the splendor of ancient, sun-filled temples, shimmering olive groves, and stony fields once trod by the company of Odysseus. The Greek soul is full of passion and love of life and others. According to Steiner, the ancient Greeks experienced the Sun as the divine source of Love. That which springs from one being to another in love is from the Sun; the human heart functions in the body much as the sun does in the cosmos. Both Sun and heart are symbols of love. Even today, to go to a market at the foot of the Meteora Monasteries in the north of Greece is to experience a social vibrancy connected to that ancient sense of the Sun as the divine source of love. It is not just that people are friendly, something we are fortunate to find in many places in the world, but these people connect with the heart, truly taking an interest in one another and enjoying one another's company—even more than they enjoy the delicious baklava and fine wines at the outdoor cafes.

There is a meditation that helps a striving ethical leader experience this same sense of divine source of love. One dwells on the heart mystery of love and hate. Love is an energy that flows outward, whereas hate contracts. Both are a reflection of the physiological activity of the heart. An ethical leader wants to give without becoming depleted; one does not wish to contract too far in the act of creating balance. If you talk too long or give too much of yourself without taking any downtime, you may end up having to do it reactively, perhaps as an outburst that alienates others. Those who focus on heart energy in such situations very soon regret the incident, make amends, and begin the cycle of out-streaming energy again. To balance this kind of unconscious behavior, we need to become more aware of the rhythms of giving and receiving, breathing in and breathing out, and the proper flow of circulation.

One way to promote ethical work is to develop a greater sensitivity toward the language of the heart. Which words and expressions carry a gesture of love and warmth that streams outward? Which expressions are cold, hard, and hateful? It is surprising to me that, frequently, the very people who profess the importance of love routinely use hateful language. It is defensive, reactive language, whereas expressions of love show interest in others, flow outward, and exhibit proactive involvement. Language can reveal either criticism or recognition, support or scheming. Ethical leaders see the spirit working in language, and they choose language that heals.

Now that we have glimpsed the Sun as a symbol of light, love, and striving for spirit, as the ancient Persians, Egyptians, and Greeks experienced it, what about modern experiences? Today, we must look for the energy of the Sun in individual human souls. Each person has gained the capacity to become a sun. At times, this fact is hidden, but we can find it when we look into the soul. Everything in the universe is a mirror; we can see the macrocosm in the microcosm. As above, so below.

It was this Sun energy that was at work in my three examples of open communication between school and community in Flensburg, Forest Row, and Johannesburg. In each place, I experienced "Sun relationships," people both giving and receiving, speaking with individual expression, yet working collaboratively. Each booth in the marketplace had its own wares, crafts, or food, yet they were arranged in concert with each other and with other things, such as the music and lighting that connected them. The people were offering the products of their labor, but one could see that they were also enjoying their relationship with the community.

Those Sun-Sun relationships contrasted with Sun-Moon relationships, which have a different quality. As you listen to a lecture, sit in a course at school, or read a book, you are receiving reflected light, but those relationships are more passive. The giving is from a more distinct source, and you receive it, just as the Moon receives the sunlight.

The central challenge of community development is to move from the Sun-Moon relationship to a Sun-Sun relationship. This means (using the school as an example) reimagining the teacher-parent relationship and the school-community relationship. The Sun-Moon is the old way of working and contradicts our quest for freedom of expression, which lives in each human soul today. When we perpetuate old forms, we provoke conflict in these areas of school life. This is why we often run into the kind of situation in which the parent who has worked the hardest, served on boards, or chaired committees will ask the most unsettling questions, and even drop out of involvement after awhile. These parents' natural tendency is to build a Sun-Sun relationship with the school, but when they are expected to stay in the more reflective Sun-Moon position, doing as they are told, there is a natural tendency to try to break out.

In my travels to various schools, this parent-teacher question is the number one issue I hear about. Let us explore this by looking at what Steiner has to say. In the first lecture of *Karmic Relationships* (vol. 6), he describes some interesting aspects of the Sun and Moon as symbols of spiritual relationships:

> What has been in operation between two human beings before they actually meet in earthly life is determined by the Moon, whereas everything that takes place between them after their meeting is determined by the Sun. Hence what occurs between two human beings before they become aquatinted can only be regarded as the outcome of iron necessity, and what happens afterward is the expression of freedom, of mutual free relationship and behavior. It is true that, when we get to know a human being, our soul subconsciously looks back to the spiritual Moon, forward to the spiritual Sun. (p. 20)

We live in the crosscurrents of past and future, between the given and what is yet to come: necessity and freedom. Wherever we bring our untransformed baggage, we are held back by the "Moon," the reflected image of our potential. But wherever we are creatively engaged in collaborative work, the "Sun" shines with new possibilities for growth. In a mediation situation, for example, I found that the group was held back by the pending divorce of two parties; after negotiations led to their withdrawal from the board, the future of that community began to take shape.

Often in consultations, I find that my chief task is to effect a kind of "release," in which people can let go of the old dynamic and find one another on a new basis. It is not always necessary for people to leave an organization—in fact, for me at least, a more positive outcome occurs with the new "birth" can arise from the dry leaves of past seasons. When we let go of the past, we also let go of what we cannot control, and thus allow the greater good to begin its work. If we cannot let go, we remain stuck and fail to meet our true lives. Many of the crises in our organizations, schools, and businesses are really opportunities for us to become more transparent to the spiritual worlds.

Let's apply the concept of Sun relationships to the parent-teacher relationship. For many parents and teachers, the first encounter with a Waldorf school is a joyful recognition: "This is what I always wanted as a child!" Or, "This kindergarten room is so beautiful; it's the perfect environment for my daughter!" Many listen with rapt attention to the explanations of Waldorf pedagogy and its curriculum, and they experience the festivals with openness. The new parent or teacher basks in the sunlight of the radiating energy of Waldorf education. Out of this comes the enthusiasm to serve as a volunteer or even take up teaching as a new career. Those who go into teaching find ever-new ways to work with the Sun forces, the formative energy of our education. Along the way, they are supported by colleagues, receive teacher training, attend conferences, work with the faculty on Anthroposophy, enjoy the arts, and study child development. A Waldorf teacher stands in the center of the school's sunspace.

The path of the parent is not so direct, and access to the Sun forces of a school can be limited, partly because most parents must work elsewhere. Parents have told me that they have jobs that are less supportive of their spiritual striving, but they remain with them to pay tuition. Here we have compromises for this group of people, at least on a soul-spiritual level, and the challenge runs deep. You see, the teachers are in the habit of telling, teaching, giving, and dispensing wisdom—much of which, by the way, is far greater than any one of us can fully realize. So teachers work with incredible content and, for the most part, enjoy undisputed authority both to dispense the content and to govern the conduct of the children in their care. Teachers follow in the old priestly tradition of dispensing wisdom. As teachers, we become good storytellers.

Yet when the authority of the storyteller is automatically transferred to the parent-teacher relationship, difficulties arise. First, parents are not children, and, as adult educators know, their learning needs are different. Adults need conversation, problem solving, and group work to move forward. So when the teacher spends most of a class night telling, with little dialogue, a kind of indigestion starts to occur, which is followed by a need to process, and if this is not allowed, the need grows into questions that can become challenges. Parents are no longer content to be the Moon in the relationship, just reflecting the Sun-wisdom of Waldorf education. They want to be co-creators of our schools. It is interesting that often the healthiest parent–teacher relationships are found in the "pioneer" stage of schools, when there is a need to do everything together just to get the school opened by September. Yet the examples of Flensburg, Forest Row, and Johannesburg show that this kind of cooperative work can also happen in mature communities, albeit more deliberately and consciously.

How do children relate to the Sun-Moon relationship? Imagine a circle of children who are singing or dancing, doing dramatic skits or jumping rope. We might see this lively picture in any school where childhood is valued and nurtured. There is joy, spontaneity, full engagement, and connection in their activities.

When these elements are present, we have Sun forces. A circle of happy, active children is the essence of a radiant Sun.

In contrast, imagine a few rows of desks in a classroom, fluorescent lights overhead, and children bent over paper and pencils. They may be doing "valuable work," and they may be learning, but it is inherently more like Moon forces. There is reflection, image making, memorization, and physical passivity. As we know, both Sun and Moon are part of our universe, and so should they be in our schools. There is a reason for both in our children's lives, for the sake of balance. The danger arises for ethical leadership when the emphasis is one-sidedly Moon oriented. When children spend too many of their waking hours bent over desks and memorizing or taking tests, they are divorced from the source of all life. They do not learn to think creatively, take an active part in their world, or develop the inner compass needed for moral and ethical decisions. Their soul landscapes become as barren as the surface of the moon.

This inner condition leads not necessarily to evil, but to a kind of pervasive amorality, in which there is an absence of vitality and activity regarding moral issues. The soul becomes numb, passive, crater-like, and will not be able to withstand the influences of outer temptations. If a school environment is simply one of Moon energy, children become more susceptible to a variety of addictions and are more likely to succumb to ethical compromises. Add to this the passive activities most children engage in, such as computer games, GameBoys, excessive television, videos, and movies, and we have an environment with no opportunity for Sun relationships.

As with a partnership—marriage, parenting, or a promising career—we need the "juice," a certain vitality, to succeed. This life force does not always make things easy—usually the contrary. The more active people are in life, the more challenges and lessons they encounter, but there are also more rewards and a greater satisfaction at the end of life. Inwardly energized people can always move through a challenge and not become trapped.

Sun energy is a quality that engages, grows, and moves, whereas Moon energy tends to reflect the surroundings and be more passive. Apathy makes it very difficult to exercise ethical leadership.

I encourage people to work with both the Sun and the Moon forces, whether in the classroom, in parent-teacher relationships, and in any work environment. I have discussed these energies in terms of the school environment, but they can be easily applied to the business world. The very nature of the corporate world seems to lend itself to passive acceptance and the kind of "cold evil" Andrew Kimbrell speaks of. Looking at the corporate world in the spiritual terms of Sun-Moon relationships can challenge the unethical ways of business in the world. Simply asking the questions that arise from such scrutiny shines sunlight into the dark corners. This spiritual practice is a good way to become proactive rather than defensive when challenged by ethical issues.

8. The Templars

"A brave man slowly wise—thus I hail my hero."
— WOLFRAM VON ESCHENBACH

PARZIVAL

Parzival, by the twelfth-century poet Wolfram von Eschenbach, is one of the great works of Western literature. It tells the story of a youth, protected by his mother as they live in the forest of Soltane. Parzival grows up not knowing his name or his heritage. When a chance encounter with three knights and a prince leads him to seek King Arthur's court, his mother dresses him in sackcloth like a fool, and gives him an old steed to ride, hoping he will avoid the sudden death of his knightly father. Parzival rides off, not even noticing that his mother has fallen to the ground, dead with the grief of her second loss.

Innocently and dutifully following the advice of his mother, he finds a lady asleep in her tent, jumps in to give her a kiss, and removes his ring, only to complain a moment later that he is hungry. He departs, leaving the lady Jeschute to deal with her irate husband when he returns. When meeting his cousin, the grieving Sigune, Parzival takes in her story and hears his name for the first time, only to leave and forget his promise to help her. With total naïveté, Parzival rides straight into Arthur's court, where, although laughed at, he asks to be made a knight. Later, when fighting the Red Knight outside, he throws his hunting spear, dishonoring his opponent as well as killing him. At each step of his early journey, Parzival is an innocent, naïve, even insensitive youth, riding along, following his impulses, and misapplying the advice of others. He does not realize the complexity of the human interactions he encounters and is poorly prepared for the reality of the world.

When we send our leaders into the world of Waldorf education, parent-teacher relations, finances, and administration, they often go the way of Parzival. This can be true of leaders in any kind of organization. Sometimes they are given well-meant advice, but rarely are they given adequate preparation. It is not unusual for a teacher trained only in our summer programs to be asked to serve as faculty chair in a young school. They agree out of love for the school and with dedication and a good deal of innocence. Unfortunately, those who fall off the leadership horse, even the good teachers, can end up leaving teaching. Some of our best talent is thus squandered. Does the Parzival story give us some hints about how to work with such leadership challenges?

Rather than aiming for perfection, the story of Parzival is really about learning to relate wisely to our imperfections. We are all ill prepared for the journey, and most of us have a fear of appearing foolish, which is reasonable; we all sometimes make mistakes, seem awkward, and even hurt others. Yet, as Linda Sussman says in her book *Speech of the Grail,* "Crossing that threshold depends on the strength to endure one's own foolishness, failure, embarrassment and humiliation ... thereby making imperfection an ally" (p. 42). Remorse, even shame, can help prick an awakening of self-reflection that leads to growth.

One cannot know what is needed ahead of time in every situation. The wise old knight Gurnemanze befriends Parzival and teaches him, among other things, not to ask too many questions. Parzival later makes the tragic mistake of not asking the fisher–Grail king any questions. Only afterward does he discover that he would have been able to help the Grail King if he had asked the nature of his suffering. In addition to knowing the difference between good and bad, ethics involves an ability to sense the right time and place for action. Leaders need to foster a highly developed sense for intuitive decision making.

No leader is self-complete. When we understand both Parzival and Gawain, we see the whole human being. Gawain's first appearance in the story illustrates this well. Parzival is sitting on his horse looking hard at the ground, where he sees a few drops of blood in the snow. Many knights of King Arthur's court of have tried to disengage him, but to no avail. However, Gawain "took note of where the Waleis was looking and followed the direction of his gaze" (Wolpert, Forward, p. 28). He covers the drops of blood with a cloth and Parzival comes to himself and is led into the court of Arthur. Gawain is the knight of sensory perception; he lives the adventures, seeks beautiful women, and notices all that the world has to offer. His outer gaze compliments the inner gaze of Parzival. He lives in the "horizontal," Parzival in the "vertical."

Every human being can strive to become complete, but in the meantime it helps for leaders to see that their colleagues complete what would otherwise remain imperfect. Gawain's and Parzival's paths cross repeatedly as they travel on their different journeys, showing that there are intersecting points where leaders can find the talent that would otherwise be lacking. When we look for complimentary qualities in others, we are in relationship. Awareness of others is the basis of all true ethics.

ETHICAL SPEECH

The Grail King Speaks:

> Let those within speak
> And dance with each other.
> Play at performance,
> Aspiring to transparency.
> And, if Pride appears,
> Sort him out,
> Appreciate his distinction,

> Then marry him to heart's discipline
> Which serves the speaking Presence
> Who returns the listening Speaker
> To the community
> In true form. (Sussman, p. 181)

These lines indicate the importance of a leader's speech in relation to ethics. The Grail King's "listening Speaker" is an odd term to those who consider listening and speaking to be two separate activities. Our everyday speech is full of witticisms, sarcasm, feigned politeness, gossip, and criticism. Many people carry these habits of speech without much awareness. The media foster such degradation of the spoken word, and language is gradually losing its vitality and connection to the soul. When I listen to people in public places, such as airports and shopping centers, I am astonished at the limited vocabulary and simplistic utterances. Speech often seems just a step away from grunts and growls. The spectrum of sound variation in speech is becoming increasingly narrow, and with it the soul's expression.

If Arthur is a knight of the deed, Parzival can be seen as a knight of the word. From his naïve acceptance and misapplication of advice from his mother and Gurnemanze to his failure to ask the question in the Grail castle and the subsequent denunciation by Cundrie (the Grail Sorceress at the court), Parzival gradually awakens to the limitations of language and the shame that come from misuse. His response is to become silent for a while as he continues his quest in search of healing. During this phase of his journey,

> the emphasis will not be directly on speaking but on perceiving; on seeing instead of just looking; on listening instead of just hearing. Eyes and ears are not sufficient. The ancients of Greece, Palestine, and Persia knew that the heart is the organ for seeing "into" and listening "into" people, things and events. (*ibid.*, p. 99)

Here we gain an insight into the listening Speaker. It is someone who perceives while speaking, experiences while sharing, lives "with" instead of speaking "at" the other. The outer faculties of speech and hearing are supported by the less obvious faculty of the heart. Listening/speaking comes from the heart.

The wise use of silence is one path to this leadership characteristic. The thirteenth-century Sufi poet Rumi describes how silence can open the soul to wonder, once we have eliminated some of the clutter of words:

> This world hurts my head with its answers, wine filling my hand, not my glass. If I could wake completely, I would say without speaking why I'm ashamed of using words. (*ibid.*, p. 101)

By quieting ourselves inwardly, we strengthen our perception, and we can then "read" people and events more accurately. The landscape is continually changing, and leaders need to be able to see into the moment, not just apply past advice or learning. We can say to aspiring ethical leaders, "Perceive in the moment, and you will be able to serve as a listening Speaker, one who is centered, awake, and decisive."

Much depends on the context of the moment. As Steiner explains,

> We must develop an ear for goodness in our speaking.... Today it is not a matter as to whether what is said is correct in a logical, abstract way. Much more depends on the context in which utterances are made, or are not made; one should develop a feeling for what is justified in a given context; what is good in certain relationships and what is not good in other relationships. We must learn an ethics of speech over and above rhetoric and logic. (*ibid.*, 227)

Thus the content and manner of communication are co-determined by the one with whom we are speaking. It is not just a matter of "I and you," but rather the "we" that arises when meaning is transformed in the act of speaking/listening. The in-between space, as the philosopher Martin Buber would say, is entirely alive, new, and vibrant. The listener/Speaker is an artist, a creator of new substance for humanity.

It is no accident that so many of our current ethical problems arise at a time in history when verbal communication has diminished, and faxes, email, and paging has increased. We see from these observations that the mere transmission of information is only a fragment of the interaction needed for true communication. Many of our business leaders have failed in the area of ethical speech. Facts are withheld from financial statements, phony "trades" are completed to make things look good, and accountants are hired to help with this subterfuge. Together, they form a "world apart" that ultimately has little to do with shareholders, consumers, and the good of the public. A bubble of deception has been created, beginning with self-deception. There is a failure to see the context of affected human beings; it is assumed that, if accountants and lawyers do not specifically identify something as "illegal," it must be okay to do it. Relationship as the basis of all business is forgotten, but, in the end, business is about human interactions.

FROM PARZIVAL TO THE TEMPLARS

It is believed that Wolfram von Eschenbach wrote his epic poem in 1212. His captivating pictures of the great knight Parzival lived in the imagination of many people at that time. The singers and poets who traveled to the various courts of the medieval world popularized several versions of this tale. The medieval soul was so attuned to these stories that, when the Templars rode onto the scene, they were welcomed with great fervor, since they combined two of the great ideals of the Middle Ages: worship and knighthood.

Founded on the heels of the first Crusade, the Knights of the Temple of Solomon (named for the place where they first took their oath of service in Jerusalem) were initially a small band of eight or nine who resolved to protect Jerusalem and the pilgrims traveling from Europe to the Holy City. By the time they reached their peak, they had become a multinational military force and a wealthy order of bankers to merchants and kings. They were given unparalleled privileges by both church and state. They owned castles and estates in England, France, Spain, and the Holy Land. The Templars inspired awe in their followers and fear in the enemy. They adhered to a strict monastic lifestyle when in peace, and fought to the last man in battle. Indeed, their rules forbade them to avoid an enemy unless they were outnumbered more than three to one. In many battles, a small band of Templars defeated vast hordes of their enemy. By the time of their final years, they had become controversial, partly because of their power and influence. In the end, Pope Clement V and King Philip the Beautiful (Philip IV, 1268–1314) conspired to bring them down, with the intent of acquiring their wealth. The members of the order were arrested, tortured, and in many cases hanged or burned at the stake.

Yet there remains a deep sense of mystery surrounding the Templars. Although their lands were seized, their treasure was never found. Did they manage to use their many ships to send it away? Did the treasure find its way to Scotland? Or did some of the Templars land in Nova Scotia? What role did they play in the revolution in Scotland? And did the Templars who survived become Freemasons, some of whom served as founding fathers of the United States? These are some of the questions that led me to explore the meaning and purpose of the Knights Templar. From the moment I happened upon a book about the Templars—intuitively at first—I felt that I could learn from the Templars' example of leadership. The age-old dilemma between spiritual service and earthly needs is particularly highlighted through the history of this Order.

ENTRANCE INTO THE ORDER

In contrast to the bonuses and stock options of today, the postulant who stood before the assembled knights of the Temple of Solomon had to promise not only poverty, chastity, and obedience, but a host of other very specific agreements. This was a kind of ethical contract to which one had to agree before being accepted into the order. Here is a sample of the questions asked of a postulant:

> Good brother, you are asking a great thing, for you see only the outer shell of our religion; you see that we have good horses, good harnesses, good food and drink and clothes, and it may seem to you that you will be at ease here. But you do not know the strong commandments that are within; for it is a difficult thing that you, who are lord of yourself, should make yourself the servant of another. You will hardly do anything that you wish; if you want to be in Europe, you may be sent beyond the seas; if you wish to be in Acre, you may be sent to Tripoli, or Antioch, or Armenia. If you wish to sleep, you may be awakened, and if you are wakeful you may be ordered to lie down. Good sweet brother, can you suffer well all these hardships? (Howarth, p. 61)

This notion of obedience and service, typical of monastic life in the Middle Ages, is worth examining further. In contrast to those entering the confines of a monastery, these knights were asked to be both monks and warriors, to work both inwardly and in the outer world. As warriors, they were under the command of the Grand Master, who functioned as would an abbot in a monastery, but they were also serving God. They were expected to accompany pilgrims on their journey, but they also provided leadership in a fractured political and economic world.

MONEY

One of the first things that struck me was that the brothers were forbidden any personal property; everything was held in common. If one person received a gift, it was considered a gift to everyone. This is similar to the sharing of food and gifts in many Native-American communities. Even personal letters were shared. Although the order itself became very wealthy, the personal property rule was strictly enforced, right down to how many horses a knight or sergeant could have and the number of blankets (two) that could be used at night. No furs were allowed, only one lamb's wool fleece, and their clothing was simple. It is impressive that many of the knights who joined the order were used to all the trappings of nobility or wealth in society, from manor houses to banquets and ornaments on the bridles of their horses. They had to give up all this elegance in exchange for their new role of service.

Going without personal property is an alien concept today. People chart their careers and plan their lives around the acquisition of possessions and wealth. It has become a cancer in our society. According to monastic theory, when you renounce physical belongings you can become master of your soul, being less susceptible to temptations of the flesh. A new kind of freedom becomes possible, because one no longer "owes anything to Caesar," and hindrances to the spiritual world are removed. This is not such an easy thing to do, and the remarkable thing about the Templars is that, rather than retreat behind the walls of a monastery, they remained totally engaged in the outer world. They became bankers, lending money and offering credit, with services rendered to noble houses all over Europe and the East. One who borrowed or deposited money in one town could repay or withdraw funds in another place, regardless of nationality. They were truly ahead of their time in working with the global movement of money.

Much of what follows comes from an interview with my father, Siegfried E. Finser (described in chapter three). To begin with, I was interested in exploring the significance of the Templars' unusual relationship to money. My father began by explaining that, at that time it was customary for a knight to take all the spoils of battle. They did not buy and sell goods or have businesses, but instead took loot from the vanquished enemy. This contrasts sharply with the Templars, who became bankers. For the most part, their wealth did not exist in hard currency, but was continually loaned to others. It circulated, which is a first in history.

The Templars were not responsible to a king, but to the Pope. Abbeys in France had to pay money to the king, but not the Templar houses. They were a rule unto themselves, and the rules of their order eliminated secular aspects. They wanted to be free of politics and divisions according to nationality, which is another way in which they were ahead of their time, and some might say, even ahead of our own time.

The Templars connected religious rule with money through their function as bankers. Even today, our currency bears religious quotes and symbols. This is part of the mystery of money; it is a purely human creation and dependent on human beings. If people lack confidence in money, it becomes worthless. It is based on the trust human beings place in one another. There are multiple, unspoken contracts extended between people as they use money to do business, and the true value of money cannot be assessed according to its weight in paper, but by mutual agreement. When a grocer gives you vegetables, you offer a piece of paper. If the grocer didn't think your money had any value, it would be considered a joke. This is why coins were originally gold or silver; one could trust and measure metal. Today, this human contract is sanctified spiritually: "In God we trust. "

If global economic systems are to work properly in the future, money will have to be increasingly connected to human ideals. One such ideal is the separation of politics from spiritual and cultural matters, and the separation of the economy from the area of politics. This would allow a freedom of initiative and creativity that is impossible today. For example, money should not play such a huge role in politics today. It corrupts the processes that should be based on equality and human rights. Likewise, schools should be primarily cultural or spiritual entities, governed by those who have talent and expertise in education, not by politicians. Further, finances are more involved in the realm of law than most people commonly believe, since money is really an agreement between citizens and their government.

Likewise, in the future, capital should not be controlled by government or business. Government should be elevated and become responsible to society and culture itself, the area in which the ideals of humanity reside and from which leadership actually arises. In fact, leadership for all three spheres—the economy, politics, and culture—is a matter of the social domain, as seen in initiative, creativity, and inspiration. Constant greed and desire for more wealth brings out the lower elements of human nature. The Templars knew this, and thus tried to inoculate themselves not only by following the common monastic vows of the time, but also by renouncing all personal wealth.

In those days, whereas monks had the usual religious duties, they also had wonderful gardens, often containing a wide variety of healing herbs. They were scientists, teachers, and "hotel managers" for those who needed it. They cared for lepers and practiced many levels of social work. However, they avoided any sort of battle. They developed a kind of immunity and were seldom attacked. Also, people were afraid of the church and its role in the afterlife. Because the Templars were both monks and warriors, their willingness to do battle and defend the helpless constituted a more active social role than was practiced by other religious orders. Their work did not take place only behind the walls of a monastery. Neither was their money kept behind a monastery wall; it was out there circulating in the secular world. Thus, one might see them as forerunners of modern human beings, who have to carry religious life all on their own. At that time, those who wanted to lead a religious life entered a convent or monastery. Today, we each carry our religious life with us through the world—spiritual life is no longer cloistered behind walls—and the Templars led the way in this regard.

As noted in the preface, the Templars downfall came when they started to fall apart spiritually. Whether it started as rumors or as fact is not clear, as they exacted their own punishments internally. But they began to have mixed loyalties in battle, sometimes helping people on both sides—which meant that, for some, they were on the wrong side. Although there are amazing stories of how they fought to the last man in battle, their downfall came not in battle but over money matters. As custodians, they began to use money as a source of power. Although they did not personally own it, wealth could be used to influence decisions. They continued to use their wealth to carry out their mission, but people began to resent the Templars' agenda, especially when they went against the ruling political powers—the kings and princes of the time.

The Templars attempted to transform human courage (knightly valor) into a purified source of spiritual power (service). Let us consider their three vows and connect them with the transformation of power: obedience, chastity, and poverty. Obedience means going beyond the individual self through dedication to a higher calling. This involves a level of accountability that is sorely lacking in many quarters today. By the Middle Ages, many of the ordinary knights had lost their legitimacy; they had become merchants, they fought among themselves, and they indulged in drinking. The Crusades were intended to give knights something to do and, in the beginning at least, were supported by both secular and religious authorities. The Templars channeled knighthood into meaningful service. Their ideal was to be free of all physical ties (poverty and chastity) while serving the common good and their Christian faith. Yet they remained human, and sometimes the money they handled gave them opportunities to manipulate events and influence leaders. This failing became their undoing, because it gained them enemies who were eager to destroy them and take over their wealth, as evident in the actions of Philip the Beautiful.

THE TEMPLARS AS
FIGHTERS FOR INDEPENDENCE

In addition to their financial leadership, the Templars were active in the political affairs of the time. They were especially interested in promoting freedom, even if it meant going against the established nation states. An example of this is the mysterious events surrounding the battle of Bannockburn on St. Johns Day, June 24, 1314. This decisive battle occurred several years after the Templars had been banished from France and excommunicated by the Church. For all intents and purposes, they had disappeared from the face of the earth.

The precise details of what happened at Bannockburn are vague. No eyewitness account has survived, and such second- or third-hand testimony as exists is distorted and confused. It is generally accepted that skirmishes occurred the day before. It is generally accepted that [Robert the] Bruce, in a classic single combat, killed the English knight Henry de Bohun. Most historians concur that the Scottish army was made up almost entirely of foot soldiers armed with pikes, spears, and axes. They also concur that only mounted men in the Scottish ranks carried swords, and that Bruce had few such men—certainly not enough in numbers, in weight of equipment and horses, to match the English knights. And yet, paradoxically, the fourteenth-century chronicler John Barbour states of Bruce that "from the Lowlands he could boast, of armored men, a full great host." From such information of the battle as survives, there does indeed seem, at one point, to have been a charge against the English archers by mounted soldiery, who, until then, had been kept in reserve as part of

Bruce's personal division. But what is most striking in the chronicles is the decisive intervention—when all the Scottish units were already engaged and the entire battle hung in the balance—of what the English regarded as a "fresh force," which suddenly erupted with banners flying from the Scottish rear. (Baigent, p. 35)

Even more mysterious is the fact that, even with this fresh assault, the English are said not to have collapsed by force of arms, but in fear of the mounted unit that appeared so suddenly at the decisive moment of battle. The special significance of that mysterious cavalry must have been recognized immediately. A group of Templars, with their beards, white mantles, and black and white banners would have elicited such a response of surprise and panic. In any case, this group turned the tide. As a result of Bannockburn, the English were repulsed, and for the next 289 years Scotland remained an independent kingdom.

Curiously, there were overtones of this in the Swiss struggle for independence against the Austrians, with accounts of a crucial battle in Kleinebasel that included knights with banners flying and who fought to the last man. The Austrians were forced to leave the area, and the country that emerged as Switzerland had, from the beginning, a strong Templar quality: fierce independence and neutrality in the political and nationalistic conflicts of others, a flag that resembles the Templar banners, and, of course, a nation of bankers. One has to wonder.

Ethical Leadership

The Templars represent a curious example of the possibilities and pitfalls of leadership. The order was formed with high ideals, and the knights certainly practiced self-sacrifice in service to others through their vows. They protected pilgrims, fought to "liberate" Jerusalem, and never asked for personal reward, as did many other knights of the time. They were courageous, respected, and feared.

At the same time, as they grew in wealth and influence, they were occasionally caught between conflicting loyalties and took sides in disputes that tarnished their reputation. At times, they followed their own star to the detriment of friends and allies. But what really undid them in the end was their power, which became the envy of kings and the very church that gave them birth. Rulers had borrowed large sums, and some feared that, without the crusades to keep them busy, the Templars would eventually take control of European affairs.

What is the real story behind the mystery of the Templars? Historians have tried to answer this, but most remain undecided. Nevertheless, there is a line of inquiry that bears further exploration. There has been a body of literature in the past twenty years or so about the Knights Templar, their treasure, and their fate. Something is attracting people to this mystery.

Those involved in the economy have the potential for doing much good as long as they serve the common good. I mean brotherhood, or fraternity, as it meant during the French Revolution. The Templars used their donations for "the cause," not for themselves, and they possessed a global consciousness. Yet it is part of the mystery of money that, as indicated, even the noblest causes can become infected by unconscious motives. Deals between people can easily be distorted, especially around money matters. It's as though evil creeps in from below the threshold of consciousness. It is a particularly lethal form of subversion, because it lives deep in the caverns of the human will.

We see examples everywhere of distorted financial dealings. It is notable that so many of the CEOs who have committed ethical misdeeds recently are overachievers and strong-willed people. Yet they seem to become victims of their money. A case in point concerns the airlines, recently in terrible financial shape and requiring huge concessions from their unions. In the midst of all this, it seems that several of the CEOs had secretly negotiated large compensation packages—pay, bonuses, and golden parachutes. When news of this came out, both the workers and much of the public became furious. The top executives seemed to have an urge that could not be satisfied, and this took precedence over common-sense politics and management. This "urge," or greed, comes from the dark places of the unconscious will, a force represented in ancient mythology as the dragon. Ethical leaders (there are some in business today) would clear their lens of precipitation, listen to diverse advisors, and consult their inner compass. These qualities can help leaders stay ahead of the situation, forge new connections, and model a higher standard than simply perpetuating the norm.

There is much that contemporary leaders can learn from the Templars, but in terms of ethics, they present the riddle of human action—service that can do much good, yet can still fail. It all depends on our understanding of human nature. What is it about the human constitution that allows good people to fail? The physical Temple in Jerusalem could not be "held" indefinitely. But is there another temple, a temple of the future, that holds greater promise?

9. The Hidden Temple

For those who are aware of a longing for coherence between their inner and outer lives, there is a dawning realization that our present culture often lacks living imaginations. Although we may feel entertained and enjoy leisure through movies, magazines, and music, their nourishment does not sustain us. People are force-fed celebrity trivia—Julia Robert's latest husband, Meg Ryan's divorce, Jennifer Lopez's body, and so on. Whether part of the teen culture or not, we get the same information through music while at the mall or waiting at the checkout counter. Our individuality becomes less and less creative. This outer speed, manic imagery, and trivial information has little to do with our inner creative world of imagination, inspiration, and intuition. These soul faculties provide the pathway that leads to the hidden temple

Why is the imaginative life so important to ethics? If one works with pictures or images that have been developed from the inner self, one has a chance of encountering the true laws of *imagination*, the authority and ownership developed from creativity. Imaginative activities—the arts in particular—stimulate feelings, balance the cold pole of concepts, and give us enthusiasm for beauty in the world. Do you really see the sunset or just let it flit by? The German botanist and writer Johann Wolfgang von Goethe spoke of a special faculty he called *knowing-seeing,* the ability to "see with understanding." In our social lives, for example, do we really see the other person, or do we just form opinions? When practiced in the social arts, Goethe's knowing-seeing can help develop both objectivity and empathy by balancing perception with knowledge of human nature.

When difficulties arise in human interactions, it is essential to speak *up* rather than down to a person. One holds an inner image greater than what is seen on the physical level. When this is possible, a current of confidence can stream into the other, and that individual will grow bigger and greater. Consider a family argument that occurs, say, over an elderly parent's needs. If siblings communicate with one another while holding negative images of the responses they expect, there is little hope of a positive outcome. If even one of them projects a positive image onto the others as they communicate, it opens the door for new solutions to old problems.

I have often experienced this when someone assumes a new task, often with considerable trepidation. A frequent question seems to be: Am I really up to this? Yet, in my experience, being "up to the task" is not just an individual matter, because, if coworkers can aim at a higher image of the person, transformation can begin immediately. I have seen people do things that months earlier they had never dreamed possible. They literally grew into what others imagined was possible. There is too much reductionism in our world; too often, we see others in their "smallness." The hidden forces of imagination liberate us from the confines of the ordinary. Imagination is the doorway to the hidden temple, our inner kingdom as human beings.

There is wisdom in ancient mythology, known to those who lived at earlier times. It is still accessible to us if we have the insight to see through the pictures to the message beneath.[1] The stories that at one time guided civilizations with their ethical undercurrent can still be explored in terms of soul development. The mythological pictures can come alive again in the soul, in the stories' interplay of the unbridled light of magical places and thick darkness of deep forests. In oral traditions, stories are told again and again, since it can take many years for the deeper

---

1. See, for example, *School Renewal* ("Devil and the Three Golden Hairs") and the story of Perseus in *School As a Journey*.

meanings to be revealed. Inner answers to questions may be carried for years, and the rewards come when they finally "speak" from the deep silence of myth. What was once readily available as part of the culture of earlier civilizations must now be sought, but the rewards are every bit as great. Specifically, those who work with imagination are more likely to have the boldness to invent new technologies, design new buildings, write new curricula for schools, and initiate positive changes in the world.

Many years ago, as I prepared to teach sixth grade for the first time, I was captivated by the mythology surrounding the seven kings of Rome, the legendary founders of the Roman Empire. I learned their stories and prepared my lessons, but there seemed to be more involved than just beginning the Roman Empire. They seemed to be symbolic of a kind of inner preparation for what was to happen later in outer history. I wondered: Who were these early "kings," and what can they tell us about ethical leadership?

The first king, Romulus, founded the city and built the walls and houses. To populate the new city, he opened the doors to all who were homeless, including migrants, criminals, and vagabonds. The second king, Numa Pompilius, established the culture and its festivals and rituals. He was deeply religious and cared about the health and well-being of the new city's inhabitants. Tulus Hostilius, the third king, was more aggressive. He expanded the boundaries, fought neighboring states, and expressed himself in vivid language. Ancus Martius established law and order and advanced the legal system—important in a city of vagrants. Tarquinius Priscus, the fifth king, stood at a focal point in the sequence; he worked to achieve new insight, but fell back onto old ways as well. The sixth king, Servius Tullius, was aptly named: he was originally a servant or, as some legends say, a slave, before being recognized for his royal talents because of the flames that played about his head as he slept. He exercised "servant leadership." Tarquinius Superbus was the last king, and might have represented the highest order of ruler had he not fallen prey to human greed and ambition. We can correlate the seven kings using ancient Sanskrit and anthroposophic terminology:[2]

ROMAN KINGS	SANSKRIT	ANTHROPOSOPHY
Romulus	*sthula sharira*	physical body
Numa Plmpilius	*linga sharira*	etheric body
Tulus Hostilius	*kama rupa*	astral body
Ancus Martius	*kama manas*	ego, or I
Tarquinius Priscus	*higher manas*	spirit self
Servius Tullius	*buddhi*	life spirit
Tarquinius Superbus	*atma*	spirit body

These kings represent seven aspects of the human being, from our most physical self, Romulus, to that which strives for the spirit, Tanquinius. The kings also represent a comprehensive social order. The sequence contains the wisdom of seven, the number that indicates completion and fullness, as represented by the seven days of the week. In this sequence, the Romans were unable to fully break through to true spirit self, as shown by the story of the downfall of Tarquinius and then later in the unfolding of Roman history. Tarquinius desired the greatness of the true leader, but could not overcome his personal ambition. In legends, this is symbolized by his loss of the ability to "read" the wisdom of the stars, as contained in the Sibylline books.

This sevenfold sequence contains symbolic relevance for us today in terms of ethical leadership. Our three lower aspects (physical, etheric, and astral bodies) can either serve or hinder free moral action. When they serve the I, or ego (which mediates between the lower and higher aspects), we are able to transform

---

2. For more detail on this terminology, see Rudolf Steiner, *Theosophy,* "The Essential Nature of the Human Being."

the given into a higher order: spirit self, life spirit, spirit-body. The I—working in the physical, etheric, and astral bodies—creates a doorway to higher soul forces. This means that we can move through a situation in full awareness and emerge with greater freedom of action. The reverse is also true; when we are unable to do the inner work of transformation, we fall back into our lower selves and become victims of our environment.

Such a sevenfold consideration is particularly relevant for modern leaders. In the workplace, wise leaders wish to promote job satisfaction among their employees. When people are happy and experience a certain level of accomplishment in their work, they are more likely to remain on the job, be creative, and find innovative solutions to new challenges. A great deal of money is spent on motivational seminars and team-building events, but consider the issue of job satisfaction from the sevenfold perspective just outlined.

First, consider the physical body as exemplified by the original King of Rome, Romulus, the legendary founder. Much of modern technology is designed to help improve physical conditions at home and in the workplace. New programs and technological advances are usually billed as ways to make life better and more efficient, leading to economic rewards and, it is hoped, more leisure time. So a leader using the "physical" frame could improve job satisfaction by providing new "tools" at work, better means of communications, and increased financial rewards as profits rise. This can help, but there is another step that can be taken.

Consider the second level, exemplified by Numa, who, according to legend, created the cultural festivities of the new city. Anthroposophy refers to this as the human etheric body, the formative life forces that we have in common with the plant world. What might improve job satisfaction on this level? Here we have an entirely different set of needs. The nourishment and sustainability of workplace conditions are most important at this level. These include social opportunities, sharing experiences, and creative team projects. When people feel "fed" on a social level and enjoy working with others, they are more likely to report overall job satisfaction. The social realm of our institutional life affects the well-being of employees in more ways than is often realized. Warmth and goodness will enhance and renew our life forces. I recall how Betty Kranis, the founder of the Great Barrington school where I taught for twelve years, often went out of her way to acknowledge and thank people, and it was always genuine. "You did well," "That was a wonderful talk," or "The children were great" were phrases frequently seen in print or heard spoken. Her leadership inspired me to stretch and do more. Even though she has now passed on, Betty continues to support me. I can see her smile and feel her presence.

One can also approach leadership from the third perspective, the "astral" element of human nature. As described in relation to the third king of Rome, this involves the emotional life—conscious passions and feelings. Tulus Hostilius represents one aspect of the emotions, since he is remembered for his direct, often brutal way of settling disputes. The key question arising from this third principle has to do with how well we are able to control our instincts and emotions. Outbursts of anger, for instance, can destroy months of teamwork and negate even the best technological improvements in the workplace. For job satisfaction on the emotional level, employees want to know: Is this a safe working environment? Safety for employees is a crucial factor in job satisfaction, not only in terms of outer security—well-lighted parking lots and guards—but also emotional safety.

Leaders can be models of generous listening and openhearted problem solving. When the human ego is able to override self-doubt, it is possible to transform instincts into ideals and reactions into vision. Where there is a higher goal that goes beyond financial incentives, people tend to give more freely of themselves. Thus, in this third realm, the transformation of the astral level leads to real ethics in the workplace. Once our physical, etheric, and astral natures can be transformed to serve a higher goal for humanity, an atmosphere can be created in the workplace that is truly moral. Devotion to an ideal greater than self creates the currency of ethics in the workplace. The three higher soul forces (as noted in the chart) can now be present with a sublime power of unity. The dollars of corporate profits can build skyscrapers in our cities, and if we work with this sevenfold path of spiritual practice, the currency of ethics can build temples.

We live in a time when the tangible, such as the Twin Towers, can vanish in a few tragic hours; but the intangible, the devotion of firefighters, can last forever. As a society, we have to realize that the headlong pursuit of material wealth is ultimately an elusive goal; you can't take it with you. But the goodness of ethical individualism exemplified by the selfless services of firefighters and policemen can build new social structures that are enduring. This is what the Templars tried to do, long before humanity was ready to appreciate them. This scaffolding of the sevenfold human being is the architecture of the new temple, one not subject to any particular religion or sect, but residing in the inner sanctum of each human being. If each of us can find this inner sanctuary within, together we can build a new Temple of Jerusalem, but this time a temple for all humanity.

> That the world is a temple, that social life must be structured and organized, and must have pillars like a temple, and that the great sages must be these pillars—it is this intention which is permeated with the ancient wisdom. That is not a kind of wisdom which is merely learned, but one which has to be built into human society. The seven principles were correctly applied. The only person able to work toward the building up of society is he who has absorbed all this knowledge, all this wisdom, into himself.[3]

---

3. Rudolf Steiner, *The Temple Legend*, p. 128.

In a sense, the story of the early Roman kings presents a character study of ethics. By examining the seven characters and learning of their gifts and struggles, we can see the possibility for transformation in building a temple of ethics. In any area where we are incomplete we are more likely to be ethically challenged. Human nature strives for unity and harmony, and wherever that is interrupted, evil can slip into the chamber of the soul, much as the snake in the tale of Tarquinius Superbus, the last of the legendary kings. In the last days of his reign, a snake often visited him, foretelling his downfall and subjection to the "fallen angel" of untransformed ambition. This legend echoes the expulsion from Paradise as told in the Bible, for it was a serpent that tempted Adam and Eve to eat the forbidden fruit. We are destined to work with the knowledge of good and evil. We cannot be ethical without awareness.

In the legends of the fifth king, Tarquinius Priscus, it seems he wanted to become more than himself, to experience the divine that lives in each human spirit, represented by the story of the eagle that briefly alights and removes his hat as he rides in an open carriage. Representing the fifth aspect of the human being, he stood at that intersection where the human I can become active within. Like the eagle in the Roman story, the human I swoops down at birth and departs at death. With this, we can be kings and queens on earth, though this fourth aspect, the I, is not truly of this world. It is our connection to the divine spark. When we lose our connection to this inner kernel, we fall, ethically and otherwise. When we work with clear consciousness of our connection to the divine, we can become true royalty, and we can govern ourselves with wisdom.

So what is the mystery of the human I? There is a remarkable moment in the life of every child when the word "I" is first spoken. Before that time, children regard themselves as just another "thing," an objective entity referred to in the third person. My son Ionas, at age two, always referred to himself as "baby"— "Baby do it," "Baby have it." When one first uses the "I," it is a truly remarkable event. Jean Paul recounts standing in a barn in a farmyard as a small boy.[4] He remembers the moment when he first experienced his Self. "So serene and solemn was this instant for him that he said of it: 'I then looked into my innermost soul as into the Holy of Holies'" (*ibid.*, 137). To experience the I is to embrace the divine in ourselves.

Looking at the seven kings as symbolic of the evolution of consciousness, we see how humans were historically prepared for this indwelling of the divine spark, and we see how humankind has moved from dependence on external guidance to the possibility of relying on inner guidance. Instead of being told by a wise teacher or guru, most people today learn about themselves and their consciousness from a spiritual practice that includes reflection on their work and relationships. The more we process inwardly, the more we become free of necessity.

In the ancient days of the Israelites, only an anointed priest was allowed to speak the name *Yahweh,* the "Holy of Holies." It was such a sacred name that for a long time it was not spoken. Then there was a shift to outer representations of the sacred teachings, which represented an evolution in consciousness. God asked King Solomon to build a temple, a "House for My Name."Many years later, this became the first home of the Knights Templar. What did the temple look like and what did it signify?

We enter the Temple of Solomon. The door itself is characteristic. The square used to function as an old symbol. Humankind has now progressed from the stage of fourfold to fivefold being, as a five-membered man who has become conscious of his own higher self. The inner divine temple is so formed as to enclose the fivefold human being. The square is holy. The door, the roof and the side pillars together form a pentagon. When man awakens from his fourfold state, that is, when he enters his inner being—the inner sanctuary is the

---

4. Jean Paul was the pseudonym of Jean Paul Friedrich Richter (1763–1825), a poet and novelist.

most important part of the temple—he sees a kind of altar....
What was represented symbolically by the temple should
become a living reality. (*ibid.*, pp. 138–139)

Steiner is speaking of symbolic representations in architecture. This is the opposite of the institutional buildings described
in chapter two—those that could not change with time. The
Temple of Solomon points to the future and leaves the earth-
centered consciousness of "four" and progresses to the cosmic
orientation of "five." Certain Native-American prophecies
speak of the end of the Fourth Sun and the beginning of the
Fifth, or the end of the Fourth World of separation and control,
and the beginning of the Fifth World of peace and harmony.
There is profound meaning in number, proportion, and ratio. As
with the human anatomy, this wisdom can be represented symbolically in architecture in such a way that it encourages health,
balance, and ethical conduct.

This wisdom—the esoteric teachings found in all cultures—
guided humanity in the past. In the Templar teachings, there is
(somewhat ironically, considering their crusading mission) a
reverence for the feminine nature of the human soul, known historically in Western culture as the "Divine Sophia," or heavenly
wisdom. Templar writings speak of "Manas," the fifth principle
of humankind that must be developed in the future. The pentagon at the entrance to the Temple of Solomon characterizes the
fivefold human being. "Four" in esoteric teachings represents
the male principle and the foundation of all things. When we
reach "five," we encounter the change associated with the feminine principle. This completeness, the more feminine principle,
typifies the wisdom of the Middle Ages and points to the next
steps for humanity. When we are living in our fivefold nature
with full consciousness, we are both earthly and cosmic, we are
complete and we are able to act ethically (*ibid.*, 145).

This spiritual path to ethical leadership is a process, and along
the way one will encounter challenges. What are some of the

struggles we find on the path of leadership? Challenges arise both from within and from without; they come from outside the school or organization, and they come from within, just as the Templars experienced challenges from the rulers of the day and from their own mistakes. The only certainty, besides death and taxes, is that there will always be struggle, and along the way, we will be wounded. I was once called to mediate a conflict between two teachers. It had been going on, at times under the surface, for a long time. In fact, when we finally got to the bottom of it, we found that the incident that originally sparked the conflict went back fourteen years! Committees, positions, entire structures had been constructed over the years around this unresolved conflict, while most of the school tried to function despite the tension between these two. In a sense, the school was held hostage to the unresolved work between two human beings. The wound had not healed but festered deep within the tissue of the school.

Consequently, I ask every school I visit to look for healing, because without it, every meeting, every decision, every school year must live with the unresolved work imbedded in it. Like Prometheus bound upon the rock, we are bound by our unresolved work in adult relationships. Once these karmic knots are loosened, the school gains a new freedom, and the life forces that can support growth (buildings, enrollment, fundraising, and so on) can flourish. Bringing the issues to the surface, engaging in mediation, is thus often greeted with tremendous relief on all sides. When there is a problem, we cannot afford to stand on the outside pointing fingers; we have to walk into the problem—into the circle. What are the tools we need for this? Steiner suggests that we begin by not judging, not lying, not taking sides, and not blaming. We need the courage to confront our own darkness, our double, so that we can step into the circle in service to the whole. Our soul forces are our tools for transformation and for contributing to a widening circle of healing.

There is a way to work with our wounds and to free leadership from the constraints of unresolved human dynamics Given the right environment, our wounds can become the gold of new wisdom. Part of the mystery I am speaking of is related to finding a sacred space, one that cannot be attacked and remains impervious to the changes in weather. This inner sanctum resides in the core of every human being, and when the drops of blood fall in that place, they are transformed into insight and new wisdom.

To reach this inner sanctum, or temple, we need to overcome the hyperactivity that plagues our daily lives and find moments of outer and inner peace that heals. The contemplative life is not very popular these days, but to exercise true leadership, we need to reclaim that ground. We need to take those inner steps that can give us clear perspective. This new view allows us to see through a challenge and not simply react by projecting our own shadow onto others. Perspective is a leadership capacity that lifts us over the hurdles, and with hands extended on either side, we can take others with us. If we engage in this journey, leadership can become truly collaborative.

Finally, I offer a few suggestions and ideas that can help us along this journey and answer these questions: How can we make a change? And where do we start?

1. We can separate observation from interpretation, fact from fiction. Simply asking for the raw data often brings the necessary material to the surface for independent judgment.

2. Starting with our own soul life, we need more emphasis on the path of the heart and less on the clever, ever-so-smart intellect. It is the intellect that can lead us into a maze of rationalization and manipulation.

3. Before making a statement, we can take a moment to examine our motivations and assumptions. This allows for a veracity test in the soul that will strengthen the moral impulses that live intrinsically in each one of us.

4. For centuries, philosophers and others have asked: What is virtue? What is goodness? We need to continue asking these questions and studying the past for individual examples such as St. Francis, who could cure lepers purely from the outstripping of intention, of love. He could cleanse wounds through his moral impulses and unconditional giving.

5. Rudolf Steiner recommended three things as a basis of moral development:

    A. Know that every human soul is divine. The belief in the divinity of human beings creates new substance for inner development.

    B. From this, one can unleash boundless love of humanity.

    C. The hope that every human being can once again reconnect with this divine foundation of essential goodness is world-creating.

6. Plato spoke of wisdom, valor, temperance and justice as the cardinal virtues. We can begin a dialogue with ourselves and our community by asking if these virtues still speak to us today.

Those who have studied the four gospels find each form of leadership represented: wisdom in John (the Eagle); courage in Luke (the Lion); balance in Mark (the Bull); and justice in Matthew (the Angel).

The leadership of the Eagle soars in the lofty heights of wisdom, gaining clear vision and ability to fly above the fray. The leadership of the Lion involves summoning the courage to do what needs to be done, out of an expansive heart. The leadership of the Bull seeks the strength that comes from the balance of competing forces. As for justice, we need to look for the leadership of the Angel, the being who whispers into our ear, guiding but not directing. When we seek to develop one or another quality in ourselves, we can use the appropriate text for meditation. Everyone has penetrated each of these virtues to various degrees. Indeed, a lifetime can be seen as the articulation of one or the other of these virtues. Thus, in our schools, we have those who bring a strong sense of justice, while others may display unusual courage by saying what needs to be said, even if it is unpopular.

Looking at the times in which we live, I wish to invoke courage as needed more than ever. Valor is the mean between foolhardiness and cowardice. The German word *gemüt* means the mid-part of the human soul, the part that is *mutvoll*, full of courage, strength, and force. Thus *Gemütseele* is literally the "soul of courage"—not military courage, but inner courage, especially the ability to act out of honesty.

7. Finally, when in doubt, act. It is better to do something and learn from it than to remain paralyzed by indecision. For example, I am not advocating foolhardiness, selling the school building in the hope that a much anticipated new one will miraculously appear, but rather, advising that you take a step, even if it is ever so small. Movement, as Waldorf teachers know from eurythmy in our workplace, has genius in it. Bring the issue into movement and see what happens.

And so all the strands of my journey are connected: architecture, child development, ethics, the Templars, and the hidden temple. My quest for ethical leadership uses a road map, but I have not always seen it ahead of time. I have traveled a way that has shown me once again how we are led by ideas, that thinking is a pathway of the soul. My journey has shown me that, in the search for ethical leadership, we need to:

• Begin early with enhanced child-rearing practices;

• Work with imagination and creativity;

• Use the idiot box only for those who think this world needs more idiots;

• Build beautiful buildings that speak to the completeness of the human being;

- Examine the inner dimensions of ethics rather than just say "NO" to bad things;
- Work with both Sun and Moon, especially the sun forces of warmth and compassion;
- Peel the onion before it is too late;
- Provide leadership mentoring for all leaders—they need and deserve it;
- Live in the sevenfold wisdom of your nature, and you will be whole;
- Join with others in building the new Temple of Jerusalem;
- And don't be afraid to serve as a leader, even if, like the Templars, you are a bit ahead of you time.

Above all, our task today is to find the hidden temple, the sevenfold nature of the human being, the pentagon within the square, the new social structures that promotes health. All our crises, from terrorism to unemployment to SARS, are there to awaken us to the call—the call to become creative builders of the lost temple, one that may never be visible as the pyramids of old, but may live in the social structure within each of us. Though invisible, it will be tangible in the ways we solve problems and meet challenges. Let our leaders be known not by what they say but by how they tap into this human potential. If we don't want to move from one issue to another, running like gerbils around and around a cage of limitations, we need ethical leaders who model the new social structure and help us all reach for something better. The Divine Sophia, Feminine Wisdom, is there to help us on our way.

And as a wonderful incentive, those who work with spiritual matters can affirm that we are not alone in this endeavor. Those who have passed on have crossed a threshold into a world from which they can help us—sometimes more than they were able to on earth. Now in the middle part of my life, I can call to mind quite a few dear friends who have died in my lifetime. Beginning with my grandmother, who died when I was thirteen, I can review my times with them and remember our joys and struggles. But what gives me the most courage of all is the feeling that they are with me, especially when I think of them. They are encouraging, at times quietly admonishing, but always supporting me, even as I write these lines. There are so many people out there who want us to succeed. Let them help each one of us become an ethical leader for humanity.

Bibliography

Aeschylus. *The Complete Greek Tragedies,* David Grene and Richard Lattimore, eds. Chicago: University of Chicago Press, 1992.

Aristotle. *The Ethics of Aristotle: The Nicomachean Ethics.* J. A. K. Thomson, trans. New York: Penguin, 1976.

Badaracco, Joseph J. "The Discipline of Building Character," in *Harvard Business Review on Leadership.* Princeton, NJ: Harvard Business School Press, 1998.

Baigent, Michael and Richard Leigh. *The Temple and the Lodge.* New York: Arcade, 1989.

Barnes, Henry. *A Life for the Spirit: Rudolf Steiner in the Crosscurrents of Our Time.* Great Barrington, MA: Anthroposophic Press, 1997.

Berry, Wendell. *In the Presence of Fear: Three Essays for a Changed World.* Great Barrington, MA: The Orion Society, 2001.

Brand, Stewart. *How Buildings Learn.* Willard, OH: Viking, 1994.

Bryce, Robert. *Pipe Dreams: Greed, Ego, and the Death of Enron.* New York: PublicAffairs, 2002.

Ciulla, Joanne B., ed. *Ethics, the Heart of Leadership.* Westport, CN: Praeger, 1998.

Collins, Jim. *Good to Great.* New York: Harper, 2001.

Evans, Bergen. *Dictionary of Mythology: Mainly Classical.* New York: Dell, 1970.

Finser, Torin M. *School As a Journey: The Eight-Year Odyssey of a Waldorf Teacher and His Class.* Great Barrington, MA: Anthroposophic Press, 1994.

————. *School Renewal: A Spiritual Journey for Change.* Great Barrington, MA: Anthroposophic Press, 2001.

Frey, Susan. *The Road to Avalon II: Cultivating Spirituality in the Classroom.* Haverford, PA: Infinity Publishing, 2000.

Gardner, Howard. *Frames of Mind: The Theory of Multiple Intelligences.* New York: Basic Books, 1993.

Hauser, Kaspar. *Kaspar Hauser, Two Essays.* Spring Valley, NY: St. George Publications, 1983.

Holt, John Caldwell. *How Children Fail.* Reading, MA: Addison-Wesley, 1995

Howarth, Stephen. *The Knights Templar.* New York: Barnes and Noble Books, 1993.

Kiersch, Johannes, "The Performance Profile of the "Beautiful Schools.'" Unpublished, based on a talk, Jan. 8, 2000.

Kimbrell, Andrew. *Cold Evil: Technology and Modern Ethics.* Great Barrington, MA: E. F. Schumacher Society, 2002.

Moore, Michael. *Stupid White Men ... and Other Sorry Excuses for the State of the Nation!* New York: Regan Books, 2001.

Peck, M. Scott. *People of the Lie: The Hope for Healing Human Evil.* New York: Simon and Schuster, 1998.

Pierce, Joseph Chilton. *Evolution's End: Claiming the Potential of Our Intelligence.* New York: HarperCollins, 1992.

Wolpert, Andrew and William Forward, eds. *The Quest for the Grail: Golden Blade,* no. 47. Edinburgh: Floris Books, 1995.

Pietzner, Carlo. *Lonely Generation and the Search for Truth.* Copake, NY: Camphill Community,

Pittsburgh Post-Gazette, Sunday, March 9, 2003 (article).

Sinclair, Andrew. *The Sword and the Grail.* Edinburgh: Birlinn, 2002.

Steiner, Rudolf. *According to Luke: The Gospel of Compassion and Love Revealed,* Great Barrington, MA: Anthroposophic Press, 2001.

———. *The Arts and Their Mission.* Great Barrington, MA: Anthroposophic Press, 1964.

———. *The Christian Mystery.* Great Barrington, MA: Anthroposophic Press. 1998.

———. *Balance in Teaching.* Spring Valley, NY: Mercury Press, 1982.

———. *Education As a Force for Social Change.* Great Barrington, MA: Anthroposophic Press, 1997.

———. *The Foundation Stone / The Life, Nature, and Cultivation of Anthroposophy.* London: Rudolf Steiner Press, 1996

———. *The Foundations of Human Experience.* Great Barrington, MA: Anthroposophic Press, 1996.

———. *Intuitive Thinking As a Spiritual Path: A Philosophy of Freedom.* Great Barrington, MA: Anthroposophic Press, 1995.

———. *Karmic Relationships: Esoteric Studies,* vol. 6. London: Rudolf Steiner Press, 1989.

———. *Metamorphoses of the Soul: Paths of Experience,* vol. 2. London: Rudolf Steiner Press, 1983.

———. *An Outline of Esoteric Science,* Great Barrington, MA: Anthroposophic Press, 1997.

———. *The Philosophy of Freedom.* London: Rudolf Steiner Press, 1979.

———. *The Spiritual Foundation of Morality: Francis of Assisi & the Christ Impulse.* London: Rudolf Steiner Press, 1961.

———. *The Stages of Higher Knowledge.* Great Barrington, MA: Anthroposophic Press, 1967.

———. *The Sun-Mystery in the Course of Human History.* London: Rudolf Steiner Press, 1978.

———. *The Temple Legend and the Golden Legend: Freemasonry & Related Occult Movements.* London: Rudolf Steiner Press, 1997.

———. *Theosophy: An Introduction to the Spiritual Processes in Human Life and in the Cosmos.* Great Barrington, MA: Anthroposophic Press, 1994.

Sussman, Linda. *The Speech of the Grail: A Journey toward Speaking that Heals & Transforms.* Great Barrington, MA: Lindisfarne Books, 1995.

Wall Street Journal, February 11, 2003, D-2 (article).

Winkler, Dr. Franz E. *The Psychology of Leadership.* New York: Myrin Institute, 1957.